Our December Hearts
Meditations for Advent and Christmas

Anne McConney

MOREHOUSE PUBLISHING

Morehouse Publishing
P.O. Box 1321
Harrisburg, PA 17105

Morehouse Publishing is a division of
The Morehouse Group.

Printed in the United States of America

Cover design by Corey Kent
Cover image: Icicles hanging over cave mouth/Corbis

McConney, Anne.
    Our December hearts : meditations for Advent and Christmas
/ Anne McConney.
        p.   cm.
    Includes bibliographical references.
    ISBN 0-8192-1786-7 (pbk. : alk. paper)
    1. Advent Meditations.   2. Christmas Meditations.
3. Episcopal Church Prayer-books and devotions—English.   I. Title.
BV40.M28   1999   99-31259
242'.33—dc21   CIP

FOREWORD

Any Advent book that attempts to provide a meditation for each and every day is in trouble before it starts, for Advent is a tricky little season that sometimes begins as early as November 27 or as late as December 3.

For those careful souls who want to read one meditation per day and no more, we therefore suggest that you begin with "Walkabout" on November 27. If Advent hasn't officially begun yet, don't worry—it soon will and you will arrive at Christmas, New Year's Day, and Epiphany right on schedule, with a glance at the feasts of Saint Lucia and the Holy Innocents along the way.

If on the other hand you are a reader given to indiscriminate grazing, may you—like the deer in the forest—find forage here for the dark time, perhaps a few rich and tasty acorns to munch, and no doubt a number of thistles to nudge aside. Graze in peace. There is no right or wrong way to read a book, for any book, even the worst, is a message in a bottle, set adrift by another human soul, and should be received in whatever way suits best.

May we know the love of God through Advent and in all the seasons of our lives.

for Janet

WALKABOUT

T he time of Advent is a strange time, a season of dark, a season of waiting. It is also, perhaps oddly, a season of movement and journeying, a season of discovery. It carries within it a powerful sense of a place left behind and a place not yet reached. Advent is filled with loss and regret and unshaped possibilities. Advent sings to us of death and birth and rebirth.

Among the native Australians there is a custom called *walkabout*. When a man or woman feels the need for spiritual renewal, he or she sets out, usually on foot, to go where chance or fate or impulse may lead, to see the world as it is in this particular place on this particular year or month or week or day, to drink the present moment in all its fullness and thus quench the thirst of the spirit. It is an ancient and wise custom.

In the Christian year, Advent is the season of walkabout.

It is a paradox that this should be so, that this season in which we huddle near warmth and light should also be the season when we open our minds to all the potentialities of God's creation. Deep in November the sun wanes quickly and the nights are heavy with a frost as cold as ancient bones. This is a time that chilled our primitive ancestors with dread, a time when the sun began to sink and fail, and who knew if it would ever come again? These antique memories, foolish as we know them to be, still ride in our genes, still shape our human legacy. Somewhere in the core of our being we know that we were born for the light, and the loss of it fills us with anguish.

If ever there was a time for walkabout, these dim and waning days of early winter are when we need it most. Let the body crouch by its fireside if it must; let it light its lamps against the dark that comes too swiftly and too soon. The walkabout that we call Advent is a thing of the spirit that wanders where it will, a letting in of possibility, an exploration into hidden places, and finally a song whispering in leafless trees and carried on the hard, pure air. "Come," it sings. "Here the journey begins, and it is long and not for the faint of heart. Here there be dragons."

Advent is the time when we prepare for the coming of the Christ child, the time when we stand mute and awestruck, as blinded by wonder as any shepherd on a Middle Eastern hill, the time when—in the words of poet Loren Wilkinson—"God let go of Godhead in a child."

This is the central statement of Christianity, the solid baseline of our theology from which all else follows: God let go of Godhead and lived as a human being. The God who created a cosmos larger than we can imagine and more beautiful than we can bear was born as a small, squalling infant. The God who made an eternity without beginning or end, who made time and the passage of time with all its ruthless necessities of birth, growth, aging and death, also came to live in time. God came to walk amid friends, companions and enemies, to watch the seasons come and go over a parched and dusty land, to know the past only as a memory and the future only as hope and fear. God came to live through—even as we do—the ills and joys, the pleasures and confusions that are the inevitable heritage of flesh and bone and blood.

This is the terror that strikes us to the root of our souls and the glory that burns in our blood. This is the question we fear and yet must ask: what does it mean to be human? What does it mean to believe that God was human too? *What think ye of Christ?*

So the Advent walkabout is not an easy journey, nor was meant to be. This journey leads into the deeps of our own being. It is an opening of portals we have taken care to keep closed, a letting in of the knowledge and doubt and pain without which there can be no letting in of the Christ, the child whose touch blesses, burns, heals and transfigures.

The Advent walkabout cannot be for the fainthearted for it demands extravagant courage and uncompromising honesty. It begins today. It ends at the manger that is not merely a pretty story but the transforming reality of God.

...TO THEE, A WAYFARER

T he time is uncertain but it is the dead of night. I am alone, surrounded by a labyrinth of dirty brick walls lit by dim bulbs with wire-mesh covers. Graffiti and a few makeshift signs cover the walls, for this is the warehouse district of a large city, a deserted warren of aging buildings tied together by an unruly knot of cobble and asphalt and cracked cement streets.

I prowl through this empty urban night searching for a way out, for there is somewhere I need to reach, some far, bright place that I must find. . . .

I dreamed this dream at intervals over many years. It was never a nightmare; I felt only frustration at a situation that, in real life, probably would have filled me with terror. In my dreams I never reached the shining place, but I rather imagine it may have represented ordination, for after I became a priest the dream stopped and I have never had it since.

The memory of the dream serves to remind me, however, that the mind is a wondrous thing and that we have only begun to scout its mysteries. The mind can take the images of every day and by the alchemy of dreams turn them into symbols of a deeper truth. And one of the most universal of these symbols is that life is a journey. We are all, somewhere deep in our psyches, poor wayfaring strangers. We are pilgrims searching for the way to God, often unaware that we have already found it.

Jesus said, "I am the way," and added, "No one comes to the Father but by me" (John 14:6)—a statement that has all too often been interpreted to mean that unless one holds the proper opinions about Jesus, one cannot get to heaven.

We need, I think, to move beyond such concepts. Christianity is a complex religion. The "simple gospel" is not simple at all, nor was it understood so in the early church. During those first centuries, the church demanded some three years of intensive study before administering baptism. The theological thought of Paul still engrosses scholars with its intricacy and boldness. In every era across our span of two thousand years, saints, thinkers, and poets have added new insights and understandings to the once-and-forever Good News.

When we speak of Christ, then, as "the way," I think we need to pause and ask what we mean by that phrase. *Way* is, after all, one of those slippery little words with several meanings, each of them slightly different. We ask "the way" to our destination; we show a child "the way" to tie his shoes; sometimes we say with pride, "I did it my way," or speak of "the American way." Which of these ways do we mean when we talk of Christ?

The answer, of course, is all of them. Christ is the path that leads into the creating mind that made the universe; he is the gateway into love and the bridge that lies across the chasm between human and divine. He is our *camino real* into the heart of God.

But Christ is more than that; he is also our model and our mentor. Just as we show a child how to perform simple life skills, Christ instructs us and demonstrates for us the far more complicated skills of spiritual living. And, last of all, Christ is the sanctified life within every one of us. Somewhere in the reaches beyond this world, we have agreed to accept the inner fire kindled in us, to take on the daunting and humbling task of continuing Christ's healing and redemptive work, to say with Paul, "It is no longer I who live, but Christ who lives in me" (Galatians 2:20).

So I suggest that the Christ life is the human life and the way it represents is the human way. How could it be otherwise? It is in the human identity of Jesus that God has been revealed, the same human identity that the Athanasian Creed insists has been taken into God.

So we poor pilgrims go on our way, robed in the ragtag glory, the tattered nobility, of our humanity, the garment we now and forever share with God. We stumble and fail and fall because that is what human beings do. We follow the vision that lies behind the sky because that is what human beings do.

We follow the voice that speaks in the night, saying in the words of the beautiful "Jesus Hymn," "A way am I, to thee a wayfarer." We ask for no more than this.

THE EVE OF SAINT ANDREW

S omewhere near the Eve of Saint Andrew I like to sit near a window and watch the day end. The winter twilight is short and comes early. The light seeps away into the west and the dark comes silently like some soft and gentle creature.

Since I have never believed that spiritual thinking is improved by discomfort—an idea surely born in drafty northern castles and cathedrals—I sit snug and sweatered and with a warm drink at hand. As the light drains from my part of the world, I begin my entry into Advent.

For Advent is the road into Christmas and Christmas is the great feast of Incarnation. We declare with song and ritual and pageantry the belief that the God of the cosmos, the same God who created the strange and spectacular starscapes revealed by our latest technology, also created a human family and then came as a newborn baby to join it. "It behooveth us to know our self," writes the Blessed Julian of Norwich, "for when we know our self, we shall fully and truly know our God." We too are incarnate—in flesh—and we must sound the depths of our own being before we can speak of how human nature can be joined to the nature of God.

What does it mean to be human? This is the single all-engrossing subject we study all our lives, the daunting question we ask of the universe and the universe asks of us.

There is a moment that is unlike any other in our lives, and I think it comes to most of us at a very early age: the moment we say "I" and then "why?" I remember when it came to me as a child, at a time as unlike an Andrew's Eve twilight as one could imagine.

The day is hot and blindingly bright, high summer with the sun in power blistering the paint on the front steps, burning my feet through my sneakers. Somewhere in the picture there are crayons, broken and spilled and melting into little rainbow puddles on the front walk. I have a vague awareness that my mother will not be happy, either about the wasted crayons or the wax on the walk, but I cannot care. I do not have time for such matters; I am engaged, body, mind and soul, in a higher enterprise.

I am looking at a tree pierced with sunlight and filled with shadowed deeps. I sit in my head like a pilot in a cockpit; I look out through my eyes as if they were windows and think *I am I*; I say it over and over to myself—a mantra, a mystery, finally almost a trance. I fall into the center of myself and find no way out. Why? What magic of the universe has placed me here? Why am I not sitting in some other brain and looking at some other tree? Why am *I* here at all? The wonder is too large to hold.

The moment comes to us all. Somewhere, somehow, we speak the God-word, the "I am," and the world turns around. We have moved across the divide between seeing the tree and "I am seeing the tree." We are apprenticed to our humanity and will be for the rest of our lives.

There is grief in this as well as wonder. We have claimed our humanity and lost the world; from this day onward we will see the tree, but only in rare and fast-fleeing moments will we be at one with the tree. No one will ever be me and I will never be anyone else. When we have recognized our own consciousness—and the consciousness of others—we have learned the basic distinction of life: the *I* and the *not-I*.

This distinction is the key to every relationship we will ever have, with human or beast or God, and the moment it comes to us, in blazing summer or deep winter, is our Saint Andrew's Eve. It is the point-instant from which we begin our exploration of what it means to be human— to live in flesh and time and the community of our fellows—and of what it might mean to believe that God became human too.

The day is gone now; full darkness lies across the land; the lights of the town are blinking on. Behind every yellow-bright window there is a human being, a life, a mystery.

It is time to get up from my chair, time to turn on my own lights, time to return to the pragmatic and practical world. It is time to think about dinner.

WRESTLING WITH THE ANGEL

S ometimes I go back and read what I have written and I am appalled. Who is this person who writes for all the world as if she knew what she was talking about? This writer who speaks of cosmic mysteries with only the refractory tool of language in her hand? She is not anyone I know.

For I know myself to be a trembler on the brink, sometimes hearing whispers from behind the sky, sometimes seeing a flash of silver like a fish disappearing into dark seas, sometimes merely confused amid messages sung in sunlight and bee-drone. News of the infinite comes through in no grammar known to us. We translate crudely and sometimes not at all.

Yet translate we must. We human beings, it seems, have opted for meaning. We have said that to exist is not enough; we must also understand our existence. We must define this place of wonder where we have, all amazed, found ourselves, this universe where God spreads forth beauty in uncountable shapes, where the cosmic Christ touches new sunfires into being, where the Spirit flows and flames and is never still. If language is the means we must use, then we will use it, though we know it to be a harsh angel met in a lonely place. We will wrestle it through the night and leave lamed and exhausted and unsure of the blessing, but we will speak.

We can do nothing else. Language is the means by which we perceive our own reality. It is our incantation against the dark as if—as theological writer Dr. Peter Hawkins has written—"to fall silent is to disappear into the void from which we first spoke ourselves into existence." Words are our weaponry in the enduring battle against chaos and the meaninglessness that always seems ready to reclaim us. Our scriptures teach that God spoke the universe into being, that Christ is the Logos, the eternal

Word. We define ourselves—and everything else—by means of language.

We not only define ourselves by means of language—we are in turn defined by it. We live our lives within the boundaries of those ideas and mind patterns that our language or languages can express. This tool we have devised—this wondrous, flexible, and complex tool made to move us beyond our immediate sensory experience, this invention crafted so that our wisdom (yes, and our foolishness too) shall not be lost, this door we have opened on a larger life—is also the door that closes against us. We have chosen to know ourselves and our world and to pass our knowledge to others. We have chosen to live by words, which means that we have chosen to live by symbols.

We live in what philosopher and essayist Francis Bacon called the *mundus alter,* which is not the world as it is but the world as it is perceived, the world tagged with definitions and expectations, interpretations and memories of past experiences, our own and those of others. The *mundus alter* is the matrix of education, art and culture, and nearly everything we know of the *mundus alter* is mediated to us through words, which is to say that it is mediated through symbols. Our knowledge of everything but our most immediate surroundings comes to us at one, and often at two, removes.

Animals share in our experience of pleasure and pain, but it is we humans who define and therefore go haunted by meaning all our days. It is we, tenants of a pitiless and intricate world, balanced on pillars of bone beneath a sky full of fires, who have become the guardians of meaning and thus also the guardians of the pain and joy of our world. We define them and thereby suffer them, not in the body alone but in the far more profound reaches of the mind. And then we do an odd and remarkable thing. We make poetry of them.

Poetry is, after all, nothing but a desperate and often foredoomed attempt to compel language beyond its natural barriers, to cajole and force and brutalize it into carrying meaning heavier than it was designed to bear. We search for the reality that is beyond all symbols with only words—those slippery and elusive and sometimes rough-hewn tools—at our command. We do not speak with wisdom, we do not write with truth, but we do as well as we can.

We wrestle with the angel. Perhaps it is enough.

DECEMBER 1

THE PRECISION OF INCARNATION

I was once seriously taken to task by a woman for suggesting, in a sermon, that Jesus might have had a purely human reaction. "He was *God,*" she said, presumably meaning that God would not have been irritated by interruptions, would not have tried to turn away the Syrophoenician woman, would not have lost his temper with the moneychangers, would not have snapped at one of his most loyal followers and, since scripture records that he did all these things and more, there must have been Some Other Purpose, deeper and more mysteriously hidden in the divine will.

She shares this opinion with some of the evangelists, notably Matthew with his incessantly repeated "He said this so that the prophecy might be fulfilled. . . ."

Human nature, simple and direct and understandable, is an easier explanation. It is, after all, just as much a heresy (if we can still use that old and venerable word) to doubt Jesus' humanity as it is to doubt his Godhood.

As Dorothy L. Sayers points out in her introduction to *The Man Born to Be King,* these concepts tend to occur in cycles, with one era stressing the eternal, cosmic Christ, another era the human Jesus. And yet, whatever era we may live in, we must do our best to balance the two. And there can be no better time than Advent, as we prepare for the great Feast of the Incarnation, to examine exactly what we mean when we speak of "true God and true man."

I recently led a small discussion group in which we asked: "What would it be like to be both God and human?" The only thing we agreed on completely was that our minds were indeed boggling!

9

After all, God and human would seem to be exact opposites. God is all-wise, all-powerful and all-knowing, living in an eternity without beginning or end, holding all creation in being. A human, on the other hand, knows neither the future nor, in any true sense, the past, is pitiably vulnerable to all the chances and changes of a dangerous planet, and even with the best of intentions muddles and blunders from one end of life to the other. How can these two forms of consciousness exist in one being?

I think that, first of all, we must begin by insisting on the full humanity of Jesus, simply because a being who could know and control all things before they happened would have few points of contact with the human condition; he would not, in fact, be human in any real sense at all.

To be incarnate is to be a spiritual being in a physical body, to be subject to all the limitations of time and place and culture.

Incarnation is almost unbearably precise. Even a few years' difference in our birthdates would mean a different set of schoolmates, a different relationship with our siblings and perhaps with our parents. It would mean the influences of our culture, changing constantly as they do, would strike us at different ages as we were growing up. (The first big, breaking story I worked on as a budding journalist was the Kennedy assassination; it had a quite different influence on me than it would have had at, say, age twelve.)

All the things that affect us, then, would have affected Jesus as well and yet, as Sayers also insists, "his consciousness was the consciousness of God."

How could this be? How can the consciousness of God and the consciousness of a human being ever touch and be one? When we put it in those terms, the answer becomes strikingly clear: we must find the place or places where the human and the divine mind are not different but alike.

And again, the answer stands out for us: the human mind and the mind of God are alike in the passion and the will to love—even to love sacrificially. The God-mind loves because that is its nature; the human mind loves because it was created in the image of God.

This is the point of contact beyond which nothing more is needed. It is the reason for the baby in the manger, the reason for celebration, the reason for thanksgiving.

KINFOLK AND EXILES

Perhaps the first essential of life is that we do not live it alone. A mammalian infant of any species cannot survive without the care and nurturing of others of its kind. Even after it becomes able to see to its own basic needs, it must be taught to do so, and the long childhood of the human species may indicate an uncommonly large need of learning.

Even after the child matures, the society of others is essential. Psychiatrists have documented the mental states of individuals subjected to extended periods of total isolation and have found them to be almost invariably abnormal. The inability to break out of personal isolation is a hallmark of most mental illness.

Somehow, then, the society of our fellows is essential to our humanity, and so it would have been for Jesus too. The nurturing of his mother Mary, the care and protection of Joseph, and membership in what, in that era, would have been a large extended family, all contributed to the humanity of the man who was also God. It is perhaps a paradox, certainly a basic truth, that we do not achieve individuation without the help of others. It would seem that the *I* cannot fully develop until it recognizes and interacts with the *not-I*.

Yet the matter goes further. Today we are more and more coming to understand what few persons in Jesus' time would have known or even cared to know: we are all interlinked in a great web of dependency upon one another. This is the concept the British theologian Charles Williams called co-inherence and which he was convinced operated on a mental and spiritual level as well as a physical one.

According to Williams, the command that we bear one another's burdens is quite simple and straightforward: we are to carry not only boxes and bags for each other but mental and spiritual burdens as well. We are not simply to lend a sympathetic ear, either—we are to actively relieve the other person by taking the burden on ourselves.

Is your friend worried by a necessary car trip in bad weather? You can agree to bear the burden of worry for her. Though she herself will still have to make the trip, she will do so without anxiety. Does your brother fear medical tests? Your offer to carry his fear can put him at peace and allow him to face the tests calmly. In Williams' thought, such substitutions are "the open secret of the saints," known and practiced in the church from its earliest days and taking their power from the one great substitution made by Christ.

Spiritual exchange or simple psychological comfort, these substitutionary concepts serve to keep us aware of the great web of life that covers our planet, weaving a single tapestry rich with color and movement.

Less than half a century has passed since we saw the first photograph of the world as it truly is, a fragile blue bubble singing its song of being against the black silence of space. We have seen that the seas wash many shores, that the land masses have no boundaries marked upon them. This single image says more clearly than words that we are all one, caught in the great matrix of existence.

We are flung out from God's hand to walk for a time on this sphere that looks like no more than a Christmas ornament, then gathered home again. And meanwhile all who draw or have ever drawn breath are our brothers and sisters.

There are, of course, exiles among us, but they are not those you think—not the broken, not the outcasts, not the prisoners nor yet the homeless. They are, rather, the self-exiled. They are those who refuse to think in terms other than Us and Them. They are those who believe that power confers right and that all the earth is theirs to use. The god they have made in their own image always agrees with them.

They too are part of the dance; God draws no circles of exclusion, and they are welcome whenever they are ready to claim admittance to the great gathering where birth is the only entrance fee and the music of kinship plays for all.

The host is coming to feast with us; in Advent we prepare to dance with him.

DECEMBER 3

THE SPIDERWEBS OF LIFE

Perhaps the greatest shaping force in the life of a human being is the one that, much of the time, we are least aware of—the culture in which we live. This complex matrix of values and behaviors and expectations and mindsets is so much an unquestioned part of our lives that we seldom think about it. Yet this, perhaps more than any other factor, governs us from birth to death.

To speak of "culture" in the singular is, in fact, misleading, for all of us participate in and partake of many cultures: religious, professional, ethnic, national, and neighborhood cultures, each with its program of shared, inculcated beliefs. The languages we speak, the foods we eat, the ways we relate to one another within our families and our circle of friends—all are a part of the cultures that shape us and make us what we are.

Humans are not solitary animals. We are part of a community, which means that we are part of a culture. Without it, we could not survive as human beings; even those rare souls who reject their cultures are, by that very act, related to the thing they reject.

For most of us, there is no more temptation to reject our culture than there is for a fish to reject water. Culture exacts certain dues from us and we pay them gladly, without thought or question, for within a culture we find safety and acceptance. As long as we do not violate the generally accepted taboos, as long as we share certain basic assumptions, as long as we behave as expected, our place is secure. Culture rewards those who conform and punishes those who do not.

And yet throughout history we see an odd phenomenon: this social spiderweb that holds us fast is also our major vehicle for change, and change almost invariably begins from the bottom up. Like a great

13

groundswell that suddenly breaks into the foam and froth of a wave, change comes with the rush that proves a great many persons were ready for it.

Those in positions of power seldom welcome change, and the young, the questioners, sometimes the discontented or the misused, seldom have the power or resources to initiate change. When a great visionary emerges to give voice and focus to their feelings, however, they follow with enthusiasm. Cultural changes often come, when they come at all, with blinding speed.

Such, I believe, was the case with Jesus, whose problems lay entirely with the authority figures of his day while, we are told, "the great throng heard him gladly" (Mark 12:37).

Jesus was clearly and directly involved in the common culture of his day; every parable he told shows his intimacy with the daily round of the villagers, farmers, and merchants of first-century Palestine; every recorded event of his life shows his deep knowledge of their thoughts, their values, and their assumptions. Yet there is no other historical figure who so completely transcends the cultural imperatives of his or her time and place. He did not reject his culture; he was, in fact, completely immersed in it, and yet he dreamed so far beyond it that, even after twenty centuries, the dream still calls to us in our madly different world.

Most of us, his present-day followers, are not called to be rallying points of great social changes nor, I imagine, do most of us want to be, as there are few more dangerous jobs in this world. Yet we can all be not merely followers of the dream but its active disciples. And we can do this not by either blindly rejecting or blindly accepting our culture, but by immersing ourselves in it as he did, by bringing each facet we uncover into the clear and all-revealing light of God's love and by daring to question old tenets and embrace new concepts.

There are, after all, no perfect cultures, for any culture that might manage to achieve perfection would, at that same instant, become stagnant and moribund.

We may dream of our Edens, our Utopias, our Camelots, even as we know they are impossible, but we follow God, the great Dreamer who forever makes all things new.

THE CALL OF THE UNWILD

T here was a year, and not too long ago, when I happened to be unemployed except for a small part-time job that fell woefully short of even beginning to pay my bills. I was frantic and battered and perilously close to defeated.

I had one extravagance, and everyone who has ever been on the thin edge of broke will know how much of an extravagance it was. I went out each Saturday morning quite early and bought a cup of coffee and a doughnut. I then drove to a nearby park where there was a small lake. I sat in the car and ate my doughnut and watched the geese and gulls and ducks, and when I had finished my own breakfast, I fed them some of the day-old bread I bought every Friday at a bakery thrift shop.

I was not, of course, the only one to perform this Saturday ritual. Young mothers arrived with toddlers in tow, impeccable old gentlemen in Norfolk jackets—and sometimes in three-piece suits—came to take the sun on the park benches, earnest joggers thumped past. Nearly all came carrying bags of torn-up bread; even the joggers seemed to plan their runs to end at the lake. Feeding waterfowl was a sociable event.

The appearance of a human form on the lake shore was a signal to every winged creature in sight; a few would even mount sentry duty beside the car. These would pounce on the first crumb and the rest would come—winging, swimming, waddling—to get in on the handout. Some of the geese were so bold that, if you didn't toss the bread quickly enough, they would tweak it irascibly out of your fingers. For a time the lake became home to a bachelor swan. This creature's head came up to my shoulder, and he had no compunction about thrusting that head through the car window and giving an outraged "Aaannk" if he thought I dallied.

So feeding these raucous, demanding mendicants became important to me. I knew why and I knew that one day feeding them would still be fun but would never be important in quite that way ever again.

The geese were Canadas, surely the most elegant of all geese with their black heads and neat white chin straps. Hearing a flock of migrating Canadas overhead is the quintessential sound of wildness, just as the crying of gulls is the quintessential sound of the sea, but the birds I fed in the park could scarcely be called wild. Somewhere along the way they had opted for the manmade lake and the easy handouts; most no longer bothered to migrate.

Yet somehow, even so, they managed to carry, however faintly, the aura of cold skies and unknown waters and the wild north, and thus they became for me a small corner of freedom at a time when very little freedom seemed available. It was a time when I prayed for the right job, and then for a good job, and finally for any job at all, a time when worry became my work. In those days I explored what it is to be unfree, not by political tyranny or by act of another, but simply by the hard reality of the world.

Eventually, of course, I found a job, though it was not one I wanted or would have chosen; it took me a long time to realize that it was a good job, and even longer to discover that it was, in God's wisdom, the right job, one that led me to places and thoughts I would never have known without it.

All that is past, yet I remember the geese and the gulls, the ducks and the cantankerous swan: the wild creatures who were no longer wild.

I remember them because I think we are so much like them. We too live our domestic lives, build our nests and raise our young. We walk the round of daily chores and receive our handouts, earned and unearned. And in the midst of it, by some uneasy whispering of the soul, we also know that we are wild and free, that our destiny lies beyond the park and the world and all the troublesome small exigencies of life.

The soul is a wild goose, flying free in the sweet clean air.

GAZING INTO THE MYSTERY

G aze too long into the abyss," says Nietzsche, "and you will find that the abyss is also gazing into you." The same might be said of the mystery of God, except that the mystery of God is not emptiness but a vast overflow of life, and what gazes back is a love too deep to comprehend.

There are moments, rare and brief, when we may see this, when the largest thing that can ever happen to us may, as British writer and theologian C. S. Lewis notes, find space for itself in less time than a heartbeat. I remember a hot summer afternoon when I had decided to walk to the grocery store for a few forgotten items. It was the sort of day that folks in the plains states call a "weatherbreeder," and it lived up to its reputation; in the half-hour I spent in the store, the sun went under, the clouds came up, and a stiff wind caught me as I came out the door. By the time I was halfway home, the tornado-warning sirens were whooping and bellowing.

I was terrified, of course (one does well to fear a tornado, a tricksy, dangerous wind capable of bulldozing entire neighborhoods). I ran home—not far, but up a rather steep hill—and arrived on my back porch panting, heart thudding, shaking with alarm and exertion.

A scientist or psychologist might perhaps say that it was my own stressed and edgy state that triggered the great calm that came then and enfolded me in warmth and comfort. I was suddenly aware of the universe around me, largest star to smallest atom, moving in a joyous and noble dance. And the universe was a living thing, enclosed within a great love that held it in being. I had come all unexpectedly into a place of perfect safety. The tornado might or might not kill me, but I knew with utter certainty that it would never remove me from the sheltering of that enormous love.

Clearly the tornado did not kill me (nor anyone else that day) but the moment that was too short to measure marked me forever with the sigils of awe and knowledge. I have tried several times to seize that experience and bind it in words on paper, but I never succeeded—nor have I succeeded now.

If I were to put a name to that surrounding love, I think it would be Logos, the eternal Word begotten of the eternal Dreamer, the Son by whom all things were made and dressed in their beauty. This is the mystery into which we will gaze for all eternity and never be tired. This is the life of the Godhead into which we have been linked by the incarnation of Christ.

The French philosopher Gabriel Marcel has written that we always tend to think of mystery as something "out there," something we reach for but can't quite grasp. Perhaps, he says, the mystery is too close for us to see; we cannot understand it because we are standing in the middle of it. We speak, for example, about the mystery of love; we don't understand love, we can't explain it, we don't know why it happens, yet every one of us has experienced it.

So it is, I think, with God's love. We stand surrounded by mystery we cannot define or comprehend; it lies beyond us and within us; it whispers in our brains and sings in our blood. Perhaps the Word was made flesh and dwelt among us so that we might experience God's love in the same way we experience human love, so that the unimaginable might become for us real, solid and touchable.

It remains, of course, no less a mystery; if it were small enough to comprehend (as has been said many times), it would be too small to be God. Mystery is not meant to baffle us; it is meant to delight us, to remind us that there will always be new explorations and new wisdoms and new adventures of the mind and spirit.

We gaze into the mystery and the mystery gazes back with love.

MAKERS AND SHAPERS
AND TELLERS OF TALES

G od is the first and great mystery but the second—linked to it and like unto it—is the mystery of humankind. These strange and baffling creatures not only insist that they are indeed made in the image of God, but they then proceed to demonstrate that image over and over again.

Wherever we find evidence of human habitation, we find not only human artifacts but artifacts made with care and beauty. A flint arrowhead is not only efficient—it carries the deadly elegance of a lethal thing. The cave paintings of southern France may have served some unknown ritual purpose, but they are also filled with intentional truth and exquisite grace. If God is the Creator—as all religions seem to agree—then human beings live into the image with passion and a certain fervent abandonment, as if some pressure of the spirit could be released in no other way.

I recently read of a study that had rated 95 percent of preschool children but only 5 percent of college graduates as "highly creative." At the time I was properly appalled; today, more pragmatically, I distrust the study itself. Perhaps the definitions were too limited, the criteria too strict; I see too much creativity exploding all around me to believe it is being produced by only a small percentage of the population.

Enough people write to keep a small industry busy filling their needs. Not everyone can be a Shakespeare or a Dante, but some will be skilled enough to keep the bookstores overflowing.

Not everyone can be a Michaelangelo or a Rembrandt, but craft and art supply stores flourish in almost every town. Not everyone can be a Bach or a Mozart or, for that matter, a John Lennon, but MTV blares, symphony orchestras tune up, bands march, children thump their way through "Swans and Lilies," and the world is filled with music.

Nor is human creativity confined to the arts; a loving home is a creation of the first order. Most business people love their work not because it may make them rich but because it gives them the pleasure of creating. Bridges are flung across rivers, life-changing devices are invented, new scientific theories are constructed, new medicines found. Planes fly, buildings rise up; from the deep reaches of abstract thought to the sweat of hard labor, the world churns busily on, making, always making, forever making, making, making.

Of all our creations, perhaps the most universal and most beloved is the telling of stories. Tales are told around campfires and kitchen tables, over rural fences and in the corridors of power. Stories seem to be the way we define ourselves to ourselves. Every good family produces stories that become private legends and, ultimately, a part of the clan mythos.

All great religions begin with stories, and Jesus was one of the great storytellers of all time. We may imagine the original tellings of those stories, and no doubt they were very unlike the readings we hear in church. There would have been dramatic pauses, voice changes, perhaps vocal sound effects to delight the children, and telling gestures, all the techniques of the master storyteller.

And what stories they are! They came, as all good stories come, out of the life experiences of both teller and hearers, embellished with a good dollop of "what if. . . ?" Had Jesus heard of a traveler set upon by thieves and left to die? What if a kindly stranger had come along? What if he had been one of the much-hated Samaritans? The parable, rich with meaning, begins to take shape.

In Jesus' world the younger son who wastes his inheritance might have come from a nearby farm. The woman sweeping her house to find a lost coin was a commonplace, the gem merchant riding to Jerusalem with his entourage of guards and his pearl of great price was a sight the village children trooped to see. It is with the warp and weft of common life that the storyteller weaves magic.

So we go our creative way through the world, making, shaping, building, singing our visions and dancing our dreams and telling day by day the most important story of all, which is the story of our own lives and which must be, by its very nature, a story of laughter and loss and despair and hope that is, now and forever, a strand in the story of God and God's action in our world.

To create is to love; to love is to create. There is no other way.

RELICS OF THE WASTELAND

Advent, the time of darkness, is also the time our Anglo-Saxon forebears would have called *wanhope*. The world is too much with us in these days of waning light and the world is old and grey and sad. This is the time of regret and remorse and lost dreams; this the time when we understand in the cold marrow of our bones that there is no surety, no safety in all this wide and barren wasteland where we wander without compass. Under this feeble sun, the spirit is diminished.

Yet we prepare to believe. We prepare to hope. We prepare to celebrate the birth of a child that our faith claims was the very God of the universe.

In the dark days of the year and in the dark days of our lives, this is a hard thing to believe. We try very hard, of course, and when doubts come creeping in, we resolutely shut them out. We deny our denials and we do so with vigor and with shame, for we have been inoculated—often from birth—with the idea that doubt is wrongheaded and even un-Christian.

Yet Advent, perhaps more than any other time, is the season that requires confrontation with our full humanity. Somehow we know that we cannot go to the manger, that place of starlight and shadow, garbed in anything less than our birthright of flesh and bone and blood, our heritage of grief and hope. We cannot enter the stable that is larger than the universe until we are willing to strip away all our old assumptions, our false proprieties, and our determined prejudices. We come to the holy to discover it, not to reaffirm that it is still there where we left it.

Doubt is an essential part of our faith. Thoreau said that "the unexamined life is not worth living," and he might have added that the unexamined faith is not worth having. Our doubts are not something to fear nor are they something to hide away in some far corner of the mind lest they be somehow improper. We need to bring them out into the strong light of utter honesty, and we need to look at them with a cold and fearless eye.

There is nothing about doubt that we need fear. Christianity is two thousand years old and it is tough as an oak tree. It invites us to examine its roots and find them strong, sunk in the rich and honest soil of earth. It welcomes us to its complex patterns of light and shade; it encourages us to shake its branches and see what falls out. No matter what we do, it will endure.

More immediately important is the fact that doubt is an encounter with our own inner selves; it is the key that opens many doors—some of which we might prefer to leave closed.

Is the factual truth of every detail important to our faith? Perhaps it may disturb us that, for example, neither historians nor biblical scholars have found any evidence of a special edict of taxation during the reign of Caesar Augustus (and besides, as every good bureaucrat knows, you tax people where they are; you do not demolish the economy by forcing them to shut down their businesses and take troublesome journeys). If we are troubled by this, we may be missing the larger truths of faith in our insistence on the details.

Perhaps, on the other hand, we discount the entire story as simply a beautiful and meaningful allegory. In that case we may need to ask ourselves if we are assuming too much about the things God can or cannot be expected to do (for surely we know by now that God seldom does the expected).

Far from being the dark side of faith, doubt is its benchmark. Doubts define not only what we believe but, if we are honest, how and why we believe it. They strengthen rather than weaken, for how can we truly say what we believe until we have tested it against the honesty of our own minds?

Ultimately doubts show us the integrity of our own spirit, which, with our love, is the only thing that—being a matter of will—is our own gift to lay before God.

LIVING IN THE APOCALYPSE

W e human beings, it seems, have a perverse habit of becoming fascinated by the things we fear; perhaps this is why the apocalypse—the end time—is the subject of so many of our fantasies. The comet will come, the meteor will strike, the invincible aliens will arrive from outer space. In the thought of many religions, it is God who, having tossed stars and planets into their intricate dance, will one day quench their light and call them home. The Zoroastrian *kantras* are filled with images of the eschaton, as is the book of Daniel in the Old Testament. Within the Christian scriptures, the book of Revelation holds its unique place.

Oddly enough, the purpose of these writings seems to be neither the gloom of despair nor the titillation of gory disaster. They are, rather, records of reassurance. The star named Wormwood may burn (and those who delight in finding current events in the book of Revelation are quick to point out that, in the Russian language, *wormwood* is *chernobyl*), but those who are worthy will survive. The *kantras* promise that, though the flames of hell may wash over all, the righteous will feel them "only as warm milk." The Hebrew children walk in the fiery furnace without harm.

According to a current theory, such literatures appear in times of crisis, times when there is a great sense of an old order passing away and a new order bringing chance and risk and uncertainty. These writings are what has been called the "dream under fire," the promise that all will yet be well.

The early Christians awaited the coming of Christ within a generation; Paul believed that he was living in the end time and taught accordingly. Now, with twenty centuries of Christian experience behind us, we know that the dream is always under fire; the dream is real only if it can be held strong and true through battle and besiegement. If we are living in the apocalypse, then the apocalypse is stretching out much longer than anyone imagined it would; all times are charged with peril.

It is small wonder we turn so readily to the past, which—no matter how troubled it may have been in reality—we remember as a time of peace and stability. We are bewildered, perhaps even outraged, when we discover that God does not allow this.

God calls us onward. God calls us to change, to growth, and to new discoveries—of ourselves, of our world, of our faith. If history teaches us anything, it is that the human race is on a tough and slow but ultimately upward path. Despite wars, depravities, and unspeakable injustices, despite lapses into cruelty and exploitation, we are moving toward new frontiers not only in the physical world but in the life of the spirit as well. As novelist Mary Renault has noted, "The Judeo-Christian ethic has changed the moral reflexes of the world." Like the frog in the well, we may slip back one inch for every two that we manage to climb, but slow progress is still progress. We do not think as our ancestors thought nor see as they saw; we condemn violences and injustices to which they were blind, just as our descendants will condemn our own blindnesses.

Perhaps the apocalypse is not a crash of trumpets and a blaze of light after all; perhaps it is a gradual process taking place all around us. Perhaps the apocalypse is not a blaze of revelation but a time of ongoing discoveries.

If so, we know what they will be: our discoveries of God are always discoveries of love, for love is the nature and being of God. This is why our journey into the spiritual life requires us to ask one question over and over: what do I love?

Do I love the past? If so, I love my own memories. Do I love certain definitions and practices of faith? If so, I love my own ideas and habits. Or do I love the God who calls me onward to new concepts and new visions of the possibilities of love and service?

God, I think, permits our false loves as long as they do no harm. Our memories, after all, may comfort us as long as we do not make them our criteria for judgment. If we need certain rules and regulations of faith, we may have them as long as we do not force them on others.

These things, however, are not required. The only call we have been commanded to heed is that we shall love God and we shall love one another, for that is the way Christ loved and still loves today. If we are living in the apocalypse, perhaps it is because all times are the apocalypse. Christ is always coming.

Christ is always here.

ARRIVALS AND DEPARTURES

S ometimes it seems that the scriptures provide us with a great deal too much about judgment. The prophets thunder God's anger. John the Baptist calls for a "generation of vipers" to repent, and Paul believes that the apocalypse will come at any moment. Even Jesus himself foretells the destruction of the temple and the persecution of his followers.

We human beings don't care to think much about judgment, or at least any judgment that might involve ourselves. We like our stories to have happy endings, and somehow the ideas of judgment and happiness don't seem to go together.

We tend to forget that there might be another view, one in which judgment is welcomed with joy. "Let the rivers clap their hands," writes the author of Psalm 98. "Let the hills ring out with joy before the LORD when he comes to judge the earth. In righteousness shall he judge the world and the peoples with equity."

This is a vision of judgment far beyond our stereotyped view: in a world more concerned with power than with ethics, God will judge in righteousness; in a world where even humankind's highest aspirations somehow fall short, God will judge with equity. Justice and mercy will stride together across an earth that has known little of either. Rejoicing will leave no room for fear.

For God's judgment has already arrived: God's judgment is Christ. And God's judgment is not the Christ of some future apotheosis, not the central figure in some apocalyptic blaze of cloud and glory: God's judgment is the baby in the manger, the young man telling stories at the side of the road, the revolutionary dying on a cross. God's judgment walked among us and made us his heirs. The more we see our lives caught up in the life of Christ, the more we will see both the light and the darkness in our own hearts. We need no other judgment.

When we give ourselves to the Christ life, we give ourselves to a life-long exploration of the power of unconditional love. We will see how such love transfigures each thing it touches. And we will exult in the knowledge that such love is not simply our temporal commitment but our eternal destiny.

This journey into life is not an easy one. It will require all the honesty of which we are capable and all the clear-eyed self-knowledge we can muster. Like any journey in the physical world, it begins—must begin—where we are and as we are, and that in itself may be a searching discovery.

We will stand before God without pretense or illusion and we will follow where God leads us to go. The life of Christ living in us will call us to strange places. It called Francis to the roads of Italy and Mother Teresa to the streets of Calcutta and it may call us also to mean streets and prison houses; it may set us to hard tasks and into uncomfortable positions. It will allow us to make no judgments except the judgment of love. And it will again and again require our acknowledgment that we are one with all outcasts, exiles and strangers.

This is the judgment of Christ that we are preparing to welcome yet again in the feast of the Nativity. This is the judgment we welcome, not with fear or foreboding but with laughter and celebration. The author of the apocryphal book of Baruch writes:

> For God will lead Israel with joy in the light of divine glory,
> with the mercy and righteousness that come from God. . .
> Take off the garment of your sorrow, O Jerusalem
> put on forever the beauty of the glory of God.

THE MILLION NAMES OF GRACE

A s I write, the snow is falling outside, great silent flakes as white and soft as goosedown, sifting through a dark stand of pine and fir. When I was a schoolchild, we were told solemnly and seriously that no two flakes were alike; I used to wonder who had looked at them all and found that out.

All different or all alike, the snowflakes are beautiful. They are also presenting me with two serious temptations, both of which I am doing my best to resist.

The first temptation is that, having decided to write about grace, I should compare grace to the snow: pure and shining, falling gently from heaven. I could wax poetic for a long time about grace being like the snow, but it would be a writer's conceit, a worn-out cliche. Nor would it be especially accurate.

I have heard it said that the Inuit peoples have forty different words for snow—separate words for heavy, wet snow, for hissing, granular snow, for snow driven on a north wind, and so on. Forty different kinds of snow. Perhaps if we had forty different words for grace, the comparison might hold good.

But forty names would not be enough to count the shapes of grace. Grace may be the constant matrix of our lives, but the way it comes to us shifts and slips beyond our reach. It is unlikely that we could have snow without knowing it, but day by day grace washes over us unnoticed. Strange and sometimes angular and unwelcome, often mistaken for a curse rather than a blessing, grace comes to our December hearts and is not recognized. Caught up in living, we do not hear the song of life.

For we are alive and God is alive, and that is the message of grace.

God the creator, the redeemer, and the sanctifier is moving and acting and singing the divine song of being. God did not create the universe a long time ago, give it a nudge, and send it on its way with a mild blessing and a "Good luck to you." God is creating now.

Nor did God redeem us once and rest content to leave it at that. Even as we live our lives, even as we drive trucks and write symphonies and change diapers, God's redemption grows within us. God did not sanctify us at our baptisms and then set us adrift to muddle along as best we can. God's grace surrounds us, holds us, and calls us into the light that is our true home.

In the end, we do not define grace: grace defines us, for we too are living and changing, moving into new and astonishing relationships, learning a wisdom we never dreamed and a life we never of ourselves could have framed. Grace shapes us and, if we allow it, brings us into the very life of the Godhead, so that we too may be creators and redeemers, we too may be bearers of God's holiness.

We human beings, as theologian Paul Tillich once wrote, are marked by estrangement, finitude, and ambiguity, yet when we come to recognize and consent to the grace in our lives, all the fragments of our being are drawn into wholeness. We enter a living process and in that process we are transformed. The human dream and the divine vision merge; the ambiguous becomes clear, the stranger is brought home, and the finite human soul discovers its infinite destiny.

The Blessed Julian of Norwich writes: "We are enclosed in the Father, we are enclosed in the Son and we are enclosed in the Holy Spirit. And the Father is enclosed in us and the Son is enclosed in us and the Holy Spirit is enclosed in us. Almightiness, all Goodness—one God, one Lord."

Even so let it be, and meanwhile the snow comes down outside, falling through the rich, cold air. The world explodes with extravagant mystery. I will give in, I think, to the second temptation. I will go walk in it.

I will tramp through this singular blessing; I will toss it with my toe, feel it on my hands and face and tongue. I wish I had a dog to walk with me, for dogs understand what to do with snow but, alas, for one of the few times in my life, I do not have a dog, and I know my cat will prefer her warm cushion. Cats have small appreciation for things damp and cold, so I shall walk alone.

Some temptations were never meant to be resisted. Snow is one of them.

ALL GOD'S CHILDREN GOT BOOTS

Somewhere, somehow, they say, everyone gets fifteen minutes of fame to last a lifetime. If this is so, then I think I had mine in the third grade. Even worse, I barely knew anything about it.

It came about in the last bleak and impatient days before the Christmas break. In those days (now beginning to seem further and further departed) there were no rules or even unspoken taboos against religious celebrations in public schools. We sang the cheerier carols and an occasional Hanukkah song, and we decked our cream-and-brown academic halls with bells and snowflakes cut from construction paper, with glitter-sprinkled stars and miles of paste-smeared paper chains.

The rear of the third-grade classroom had four inconvenient and little used blackboards and the teacher decided that these could be pressed into holiday service. She chose four students of artistic bent and gave each one a box of colored chalks and the charge to "draw something Christmasy." I was one of the four.

The picture I produced was, for the most part, ordinary in the extreme: three angels clad in garments resembling Mother Hubbard nightgowns (one pink, one white and one pale blue) hovering over a lumpy and featureless landscape in which the town of Bethlehem—complete with star—huddled in the distance.

The angels had their mouths open and were obviously singing lustily from a large sheet of music they held spread before them. I was rather pleased with myself for having managed to get six wings into a limited space, less pleased that the angels were forced, by artistic necessity, to sing with their backs turned toward Bethlehem. I figured, however, that this was okay because they were singing to the world at large. Mary and Joseph already knew about the baby.

If I had left it there, it would have remained only a child's half-formed dream of Christmas, but I did not. There was something wrong with the picture and, with the hardheaded literalness of an eight-year-old, I recognized it at once. The angels had no feet. I promptly gave them two apiece. That this was cause for comment became evident a few days later when a friend of my mother casually informed her, "I was at Park School today and saw your daughter's picture of the angels with combat boots."

My mother, who had probably been prepared to take a modest pride in her offspring's artistic achievement, was bemused by this. "Combat boots?" she asked me.

And combat boots they were, I suppose—large and brown and laced up the front—but at that time and place and era they were also common winter wear for nearly everyone, including schoolchildren. I had no explanation beyond the obvious truth that if God created angels, God would surely not have neglected to provide them with feet and with appropriate footgear. December, as surely God would know, was no time to be flying around the sky barefoot.

My mother's next suggestion—"Why didn't you just make the robes a little longer?"—carried absolutely no weight with me at all. I knew from experience that a too-long robe was likely to tip you flat on your face—an unseemly position for an angel in the act of proclaiming glad tidings.

So the angels remained, boots and all, and in those last days before the Christmas break they achieved a limited but distinctive fame. Not only the faculty and staff of my own school but a trickle of visitors from elsewhere managed to set aside legitimate business long enough to visit the third-grade classroom and view the angels with large brown boots showing beneath their pastel gowns. A modest amount of word of mouth kicked in and spread the news.

I knew little of this at the time, nor would I have cared. It was some years before I discovered the seasonal merriment my angels had provided, and even longer before I realized that I was probably carefully protected against knowing that my angels were being laughed at. This last, though kindly, was completely unnecessary. I would have gone to the mat for my angels, in the unshakable third-grader conviction that I was right in the matter of angelic feet and the need for boots. I would not have used the term *artistic integrity,* but at some gut level I knew what it was.

So what is the moral of this holiday tale? What profound lesson is to be learned from it? Probably there is none at all. Those who insist on such things, however, are welcome to contemplate angels in combat boots, third-grade imaginings, and all the other unlikely miracles and sweet absurdities of life that tangle and throw down all our certainties, undo all our pomposities, and bless us with the holy gift of laughter.

WALKING INTO THE DARK

There is a sense in Advent of huddling together, of a great darkness in which we wait, clutching as much warmth as we can manage around us like a worn-out shawl. We cry out in the silence of our hearts for God to come into our threadbare lives, for somehow we sense that only God can save us. God does not come. We long for the light but no light shines.

Humankind is not a patient species; we do not wait readily or without protest. Only we of all creatures, it would seem, are aware of our own mortality and with it the passage of time. For us the sands do not remain in the hourglass but trickle and gush and flow away. We know the desolation of loss because only we of all creatures are aware that the past does not come again.

So perhaps the greatest frustration we feel in our attempts to live the life of the spirit comes when we are forced to acknowledge that God's time is not our time. The Being we worship sits in eternity and seems not to hear us battering against the gates of mortality. God has all the time there is, but we do not; for us the biblical phrase "in the fullness of time" is a mockery.

God lives in eternity and therefore God is present—fully present—in all times and places. There are no secrets kept from God.

There are many secrets kept from human beings, though, and the largest secret of all is the future. An essential of the human condition is that we are continually walking into the dark. We live our lives in the ambivalence of uncertainty, and a large part of our spirituality depends on the courage and determination and faith with which we deal with time, the world, and a life lived without access to either past or future.

As it is for us, so it must have been for Jesus; a humanity free of such limitations is not humanity at all. We are told, for example, that when Jesus heard of the arrest of John the Baptist "he withdrew into Galilee" (Matthew 4:12)—the prudent and predictable response of an intelligent man in an uncertain and possibly volatile situation. Jesus was, after all, preaching much the same message as John, and preaching it more compellingly and rigorously. It was a message just as unpopular then as it would be if it were truly preached today: "Turn back. Repent and return to God. You will be forgiven, you will be welcomed, you will be received with joy, *but you must* sell all you have and give to the poor and walk away from all your treasure."

Among the rich and powerful, this was not a popular message. The fact that the people "heard him gladly" made it a revolutionary—and therefore a dangerous—one. Jesus needed no divine foreknowledge to know that he was placing himself in peril.

Yet he continued to teach and preach and walk the hot and common roads, and the crowds came. He preached to the poor that we are all poor, to the rich that we are all rich, to the powerful that the only true power comes from God, to the servants and slaves that we all serve one another.

Nothing tells us more about the human life of Jesus than this: he walked into the darkness of his own future with fortitude and commitment and faith. He not only brought the light of God to humankind but he took, as the Athanasian Creed says, "the manhood into God."

Even today, twenty long and hard centuries later, we are his heirs, and this is the legacy he has left us to carry on: that as the candle receives light so that it may give light, so do we receive the light of Christ—not so that we may live good and harmless lives, but so that we may continue the work of justice and love begun two thousand years ago and not finished yet.

We gather the light, we take it forth to those we love, to our communities, and finally to all the world, and the darkness shall comprehend it not.

OUR FABLES BROKEN

W hen Dante spoke of the place where all our fables are broken, he spoke a great truth of the spiritual life. We human
creatures love to make up fables and then believe in them,
and until they are broken, until we can move past them into the clear
realities of life and faith, we must remain mired in what are, in truth,
only pretty stories.

One of the most pervasive fables of Christianity is that it is . . . well,
that it is nice. Not glorious, not joyful, not transformative, but simply
nice. We have turned the exuberant and sometimes irascible Jesus into,
in British writer Dorothy L. Sayers' phrase, "a fit companion for elderly
ladies and meek curates."

Now I do not entirely agree with Sayers, in that I have known pre-
cious few meek curates, and elderly ladies are, as everyone knows, among
the most tough-minded creatures on the planet. Still, the charge is a
good one. We have all too often made in our minds a Jesus who never
was. Abetted by a popular culture that equates spirituality with a soft
voice and misty eyes, we tend to turn away from the so-called hard
gospels in favor of the easier stories. We prefer the Jesus who loved children and healed the sick to the Jesus who condemned the wicked, called
for repentance, and drove out the moneychangers with a whip.

Yet we belong to a religion that declares that the most important
question in our lives is "What think ye of Christ?" We are not going to
think truly and clearly unless we accept the hard Christ as well as the
gentle, the fiery Christ as well as the meek, and the living Christ as well
as the Christ who was born and died two thousand years ago. And we
must find him within our own lives, for if we do not find him there, it is

unlikely that we will find him anywhere else.

I confess that I have very little patience with the idea that Christ is found only inside the doors of a church; once we allow ourselves that idea, we're well on our way to having what a friend of mine calls "God in a Box," and that, of course, is wonderfully convenient. We can take out the box on Sunday morning and have ourselves a bland bit of religion, and then we can put the box back on the shelf for another week.

But God has a way of not staying in the box. God is—as the scriptures tell us again and again—the lord of life, all of life. Once we allow Christ into our lives, the chances are that we're in for a fast and bumpy ride. After all, this is someone who went where many people—then as now—would fear or disdain to go. He went into the desert, he went into the houses of outcasts; he rambled along the seashore and dined with publicans and sinners. He gathered a ragtag gaggle of fishermen and tax collectors and other socially incorrect people as his followers. He was an inveterate borrower of boats and donkeys and, at least once, of a little boy's lunch.

He went among lepers and he went among the demon-possessed and he went into the tomb and brought Lazarus out of it. In short, he went wherever he had to go and did whatever he had to do to spread the good news of God's love and God's justice.

And if we don't watch out, he'll have us doing it too. He will set us walking and talking and doing things for his sake we might never have thought possible. He is the lord of life, and wherever there is life, in the streets, in the towns, on the highways, on the sea—that is where he is. If we do not find Christ in our own world and time, we will not find him at all.

And (let us be honest) there are times when we don't want to find him. We would rather live our own lives, quietly and comfortably and without surprises. We don't want to be disturbed. But even as we close our doors and shutter our windows, we know that we will indeed be disturbed. We will be called out on a cold day because someone needs us. We will put in another hour or two at our work because someone needs us. We will sit up through the night because someone needs us.

We will do all these things because we have heard the word of Christ, and we know that this is the way the world is redeemed—not by some mighty fiat of God but strand by strand and thread by thread in daily life and by the joining of the human and divine will.

THE MOONFOOL AND THE DRAGON SONGS I

The mooncalf fool went out one day, for he had heard of a dragon that sang and he was minded to seek it out and hear it. He put on the sword that had been his father's and the helmet that had been his mother's and he strapped on such odd bits of armor as he could find lying around the house, and he went forth to find as much truth and excitement and glory as might fall into his path.

He walked through the sweet wild world and he saw many wonders and glorious sights, but not one dragon did he find. At last he came to a place where the road branched in two directions, and there between the branches was a great grey tabby cat, lying on its chest with its paws tucked under, gazing with great concentration at a blade of grass.

"O cat," said the moonfool, "which of these roads will take me to the dragon that sings, for I greatly desire to find it."

"Indeed you are a moonfool," said the cat, "for all dragons sing and all roads sooner or later lead to a dragon. Take whichever way you will."

"Then, cat," said the moonfool, "will you give me a blessing?"

"I give no blessings," said the cat, "but I will give you advice. You must not be a rabbit. You must be a cat."

The moonfool waited a time to see if the cat would care to explain itself further but, being a cat, it did not, so he bowed to it (for he had been taught to be polite). The cat did not notice, however, having watched the blade of grass so intently that it had fallen asleep. So the moonfool went his way and was much puzzled.

Before he had gone very far, however, he heard the sound of a loud and beautiful voice and it was singing a melody that made his very bones ache with longing.

It sang of fear and pain, of anguish by day and terror by night, until he wanted to fall to the ground and pull down the sky to hide him. Yet when he thought he could bear no more, it also sang of a safe place where all was peaceful and sure and no harm could come upon him. "Come into my stronghold," sang the dragon. "Abide by my ways and you will be one of the chosen, safe though the rest of the world perish."

"That is an odd way of looking at it," said the moonfool, though he was so frightened his voice sounded like the croak of a very small frog. "How do I know what your ways are?"

"I will tell you when the time comes," sang the dragon.

Now despite what he was called, the moonfool was a clever lad and he remembered the words of the cat. "I will not be a rabbit," he said, "nor act from fear. Many a coney has run from fear and into a snare." And he prudently backed away from the dragon and went his way.

Presently he came to another branch in the road and there sat a great marmalade cat with his tail wrapped around his four white paws.

"O cat," said the moonfool, "I have met your fellow feline and a dragon that sang, though its song was not for me. But I still do not know how to be a cat."

"Indeed you are a moonfool," said the cat. "You are a cat when you maintain your own ways before the world. And if you seek another dragon, then take whatever road you will."

"Then, cat," said the moonfool, "will you give me a blessing?"

"I give no blessings," said the cat, "but I will give you advice. You must not be a horse. You must be a cat."

As he left, the moonfool wished he had asked more, but when he looked back, the cat was licking a paw in a way that clearly required its entire attention, so he went on again. Soon he heard the singing of a second dragon, and its song made his very blood cry out with longing.

This dragon sang of glory, of great deeds and of battles won. "Come fight my worthy battles," sang the dragon, "and you will be among the chosen, remembered when all others are forgotten."

"That is an odd way of looking at it," said the moonfool. "How shall I know your battles are worthy?"

"I will tell you so," said the dragon.

Then the moonfool remembered the words of the cat. "I will not be a horse," he said, "to be galled by another's harness." And he prudently backed away and took to the road again.

Now that is not the end of the story, for there are many dragons and the moonfool had not yet met the worst of them. But pages run short, and, alas, the rest of the story will have to wait until next time.

THE MOONFOOL AND
THE DRAGON SONGS II

Now the moonfool went his way in the world and saw nothing common there at all. He saw seas of water and seas of sand and seas of grass, mountains rising like clouds and clouds lowering like rivers. And one day he came again to a branching of the road and there, lying at ease, was a great black cat with a white vest and golden eyes.

"O cat," said the moonfool, "I have met two others of your kind and I have heard two dragons sing songs that were not for me. But I still do not know how to be a cat."

"Indeed you are a moonfool," said the cat. "You are a cat when you call no one master. And if you seek another dragon, you will find one, for they wait down every road. Take whatever way you choose."

"Then, cat," said the moonfool, thumping down his helmet and hitching up his sword belt, "will you give me a blessing?"

"I give no blessings," said the cat, "and the time for advice is not yet come. But I will journey with you." And with that he leaped up and arranged himself around the moonfool's neck like a furry and remarkably hot collar. Soon he began to hum like a huge bumblebee, so loudly that the moonfool wondered if he would hear another dragon even if it were standing next to him.

He need not have feared, for the next dragon's song was the loudest and most beautiful of all, and it made his very heart feel as if it would burst with longing. It sang of peace and rest and an end to doubts, of final answers and an end to searching. "Come into my place of peace," sang the dragon, "and I will give you the truth that saves though all others be lost."

"That is an odd way of looking at it," said the moonfool. "How shall I know that your truth is all the truth there is?"

"I will tell you all you need to know," sang the dragon, "for more might trouble you. Come rest with me and never search beyond the hills again."

When he heard this, the moonfool felt warm tears come into his eyes and he understood how tired he was of the long roads and the chill nights and the days of endless quest. He thought of the weight of the sword that had been his father's and the helmet that had been his mother's; he also thought of the hot and prickly cat around his neck and its habit of keeping its place by digging its claws into his shoulder, and he wanted nothing more than to put them all off and live in the dragon's cool cave forever.

Then the cat leaped down with a flick of his tail that woke the moonfool from his dreaming. "The time has come for advice," said the cat, "so I will advise you. You must not be an inchworm. You must be a cat."

"Yes, I understand," said the moonfool, who was beginning to be quite good at reading cat riddles. "I must not measure myself against a twig when I might measure myself against the breadth and height of eternity." Then they both prudently backed away from the dragon and took to the road again.

After they had walked for a time, the moonfool said. "I have found that I am not a rabbit nor a horse nor an inchworm. But I still do not know how to be a cat."

"Poor moonfool," said the cat. "You are a cat when you are curious without apology and dare to make yourself at home in the universe. And now you must go on, for you have found dragons, and you have also found that dragons were not what you were truly seeking. The search never ends."

"Will you come with me, cat?" said the moonfool.

"No," said the cat, "for your kind dream on their feet and with their hands and their dreams rise up as cities and symphonies. But my kind dream in the warm sun of fat, slow mice and ancient magical lands and other things you do not know."

So they parted, and the moonfool went back to walking the world's roads again. He walked near precipices and knew himself to be safe, he fought and won great battles that no one but he ever knew about, and he heard the truth sung in many ways by many voices.

As for the cat, it returned to its place where the roads meet, and it dreamed its dreams amid the sweet-smelling grasses in a warm patch of sun. They were both of them quite content and, as far as I know, they still are.

SONG OF THE SALMON

I n an out-of-the way corner of a country that is today part of Turkey, archaeologists have evacuated a small fourth-century village. In his book *The Shape of the Liturgy,* Dom Gregory Dix has told the story of what they found there—a tiny Christian cemetery and in that cemetery a weathered gravestone. Hacked on it in the rather crude Greek of that day are the words:

HERE SLEEPS THE BLESSED CHIONE
WHO HAS FOUND JERUSALEM BECAUSE SHE PRAYED MUCH.

We will probably never know more about Chione. Except for the fluke that preserved her gravestone against the accidents of time, we would never have heard of her at all. We can assume that she was a peasant woman and, if so, that her life was harder and barer and more ungraced by comfort and beauty than we can imagine. Her world was harsh and sometimes cruel, and for her there would have been no escape from an endless round of labor. We may hope that she found a kindly husband and bore loving children, that she lived long and watched her sons and daughters bringing their own babes to lie in her lap, but we cannot know. We can surmise that she was born and baptized and lived and died all in that same small village.

We know her name and that she prayed much. We know that her family, friends, and neighbors, all those who shared the harsh and obscure life of that village, believed she had found Jerusalem.

I like to think of Chione, especially in the time of the great Christian feasts. For me she has come to symbolize our twenty centuries of Christian life, much of it a secret hidden in the heart of God. Chione is only one of the millions that make up the great cloud of witnesses, all the souls over all the years who have found Jerusalem because they prayed much. They are the compass needle that swings unerringly to the true north. They are the salmon—symbol of wisdom in a half-dozen divergent cultures—that returns strong and sure to its home.

Chione and all those like her were Christians. That is often all we know about them. Perhaps it is all we need to know.

A story is told about the medieval theologian Thomas Aquinas; it is said that on his first day at the university, he asked the question no one then or since has been able to answer. "Why?" asked young Thomas. "Why is God?" This is the question that echoes in every other. Why is this world? Why are we? Why has this mystery brought us to this particular time and place in this particular way?

Why is a Christian?

Not, what is a Christian? For that we might find many answers, some better and some worse, some glib and some beautiful.

Why is a Christian? Why has God chosen incarnation—the birth in Bethlehem, the years on the dusty roads, the death on Golgotha—to declare a message to the world? It is a mystery and yet one we must look at carefully, one we may never cease trying to solve. Paul says that we are baptized "into his death" (Romans 6:3) and, if into his death, then also into his life. We are joined, and joined forever, to the life of the Godhead.

And we are not alone. The disciples live that life with us, the blessed Chione lives that life with us, all those gone before us live that life with us, all linked in the great web that the theologian Charles Williams called "coinherence," all taking, all giving, in a mutual passion of love and strength and joy.

One day, I think, we will see the intricate weavings of this tapestry spread out in all its beauty. We will see the Christian mystery and, since not all salmon swim the same stream, we will see all the other mysteries (Why is a Jew? Why is a Muslim? Why is a Buddhist? Why is a Hindu?) as well. We will see the intermeshing of the divine will so that, as Paul says, "God may be all in all."

It has been said that the Godhead has only itself to give—but with what reckless generosity it is given! God gives God's own self and, somewhere in the depths of that mystery, we are given our own selves as well—everything we are and everything we were meant to be, habited in light and afire with love.

THE MIRACLEWORKER
AND THE PIGS

I n the long, dark weeks before Christmas, we make our plans for a miracle.

We intend to enjoy every minute of it and how could we not? Christmas is such a delightful miracle, such a cozy miracle. We see the picture everywhere we turn, in reproductions of the Old Masters, in plastic figures on our neighbor's lawn, in church pageants filled with preternaturally solemn children. Surely the most determinedly dour old Scrooge must melt before so many images of the mother and her new-born, snug in their bed of straw and guarded by Joseph, their strong, wise protector. Even the beasts have their stories here—the donkey that carried God's mother, the cat that purred the holy child to sleep, the lamb snuggled in the arms of a shepherd.

There is no hint here of the dank cold of a stable-cave, straw that goads and prickles even through fabric, the stench of manure, or the splinters of rough-hewn wood. On this night of all nights we want to believe in miracles, and we want to believe all miracles are like this one—warm and cozy and bright and welcome.

In fact, most of them are not.

The Gospels are filled with miracles, and often they are miracles with most unpleasant ramifications. After at least one of Jesus' miracles, he was forced to flee a mob intent on making him king; the blind man who received his sight was harassed by the religious authorities; several scholars have suggested that the raising of Lazarus was omitted from the first three Gospels in order to protect him and his family. Miracles are born in fear and need and seem to end, often enough, with troubles, bewilderment, and various bureaucratic problems.

Two such miracles, miracles in the midst of despair, occur back to back in the fourth and fifth chapters of the Gospel of Mark.

The first, of course, is the storm on the Sea of Galilee. Even the disciples, some of them fishermen who have ridden out many a squall, are terrified. They cry out, "Lord, we are perishing!" It is the authentic voice of terror, still ringing over twenty centuries. And Jesus wakes and calms the storm.

The second miracle tale tells of the madman in the land of the Gadarenes, a man possessed by so many demons that they say their name is "legion." Jesus again reaches out, the demons flee into the pigs, and the pigs dash over the cliffs and are drowned. The madman is cured.

And the Gadarene swineherds have lost their pigs.

I always wonder how we would have felt if we were those swineherds. It's a quiet evening. The pigs have settled down, the madman who raves and screams around the area is for once quiet, and despite a little wind and rain, it's a more peaceful evening than most we've seen.

And then suddenly, without any warning, all the pigs go crazy. They rush away, screaming and oinking, over the edge of the bluff. Down below we see them thrashing and struggling in the water. Perhaps we run down and try to pull some of them out—but they will not come. They are insane with something we cannot understand, and soon all of them are dead.

Is it any wonder the swineherds ran away? Is it any wonder the Gadarene landowners thought it would be nice if Jesus went away and performed miracles somewhere else?

You see, miracles are messy. They erupt like explosions into our careful lives. They destroy our pigs and our proprieties. They change our ideas about the way the world ought to be. They remind us that God is neither comfortable nor controllable, that God is, in fact, quite prone to do the unexpected.

Most of us are comfortable people living comfortable lives. We like to be in control and we like to know what to expect. Like the good, careful Gadarene swineherds, we keep our pigs in order. It's only when we're desperate and have nowhere else to turn—when the boat is sinking beneath our feet, when the inner darkness becomes too much to bear—that we cry out for a miracle. Most of the time we don't want one. A miracle might change us; a miracle might make us think new thoughts in new ways.

But the fact is that the miracle has already happened. The sweet and warm miracle of the baby in the barn is also the unsettling miracle that turned the world around and sent it rushing and roaring, leaping and laughing, in another direction.

Somehow the human race cried out, "We are perishing," and God replied, "Peace—be still." Somehow we all cried, "Lord, we are lost in raving darkness," and God said, "Be healed." The miracle has happened; God has come and we have been changed and saved and made whole.

We and all the world have been made new.

GIVING FAILURES

One day when I was very small and kept abed by some ubiquitous childhood disease, my grandmother taught me to knit. She arrived in my room with needles and yarn, and though she was not by nature a patient woman, she spent the better part of her morning demonstrating the basic knit stitch: needle in . . . yarn over . . . pull through. She did not leave until I had mastered it.

For a long time it was the only stitch I could do; I simply had not acquired the motor skills to deal with cabling or bobbles or even the simple purl. (Even today it is the knit stitch I find most soothing, a mindless rhythm to occupy the fingers while the mind sings and soars.)

Though I had no idea of such intricacies as the seed stitch or the trinity stitch, simple knitting was, all by itself, enough to fascinate me. Even when I had recovered from the chicken pox or measles or whatever malady had been the occasion of my learning, I continued to knit. Unable to experiment with pattern, I made do with color; every scarf and pot holder was banded with various hues.

The result was often quite remarkably ugly.

I do not recall exactly how I came to realize this bitter truth; since I gave each of these disagreeable objects away as soon as it was completed, perhaps some unlucky recipient flinched. However it came about, I suddenly saw my pot holders not as they were intended to be but as they really were: lumpy and misshapen things irregularly streaked with garish, clashing colors. Hope met reality and reality won.

Of course I took the problem to my grandmother, who proved less than sympathetic. "Everything I make's got at least one mistake," she said. "I hope nobody notices, but if they do then they do. If you wait for it to be perfect, you'll never give anything away."

Her words came back to me in the first year of my priesthood. I had made a mistake. Never mind that in the scheme of things it made no difference at all; I was convinced it would haunt me forever. I was a failure almost before I had begun. I took my woe to an old, experienced priest, hoping that he would reassure me that somehow life would go on.

He only smiled. "Just remember," he said, "that Jesus didn't do all that well either."

And he was right. Read through the four Gospels sometime (as I did) and read them as real events that happened not to "Bible characters" but to real people leading real lives. Forget the interpretations ("He said this to show . . .") and just read the facts as they are presented; you'll see our Lord making any number of miscalculations and a few real mistakes.

I find this enormously reassuring. He was human, "a reasonable soul and human flesh subsisting." Not God visiting this world in disguise. Not God dressed up as a human being like a Halloween child dressed up as a pirate. A completely *human* human being, the product of a carpenter's family, the product of a small, unsophisticated town, the product of a religion that had already proven its genius and a culture that had not. He was all these things—and somehow he was also the God of the universe. Somehow the substance of an omniscient God was linked with the substance of a fallible human being and became, as the Athanasian Creed insists, "though he be God and man yet he is not two, but one Christ."

He shares our humanity and shares it to the fullest degree. He knew the bewilderments, the fears and joys, the burning regrets, and the impossible hopes that are the inheritance of humankind. He too came to understand, as we must, that the human condition does not permit perfection, but even the hardest journey may end in joy, and angels sing over barns as well as palaces.

In this Advent time, then, let us give our failures and receive the failures of others, with a rueful inward smile, perhaps, but also with delight. The human condition may not permit perfection, but it permits love, laughter, joy, and adventure.

And surely these are enough.

THE CHILDREN AT THE GATE

In "Ash Wednesday," T. S. Eliot speaks of "the children at the gate, who will not go away and cannot pray."

As far as the second part of that phrase goes, it might refer to all of us, for there are times in every human life when prayer seems not only meaningless but impossible. At such times we wander in the badlands of the spirit, searching amid the witless babble of existence for the water of life and finding only dust.

When this happens many may fade into the distance, ashamed of their own beggary, but others, like the children at the gate, refuse to go away. Whatever their troubles of body, mind or spirit, they lay siege to heaven; they demand that God pay attention and then settle themselves down to wait. There is more than one kind of prayer.

There is little doubt that Jesus had a soft spot in his heart for the children at the gate. Over and over again in the Gospels we meet them, shameless and proud and brash as sparrows. They brazenly cut holes in a roof to lower a sick friend or scramble after Jesus on their hands and knees amid the dirt and refuse of the street.

The Syrophoenician woman is ready to face any insult—and cleverly turn it to her advantage—if only she can save her dying child; the blind man who receives his sight refuses to give in to those who doubt his miracle. Among the disciples, Peter declares, "To whom shall we go? You have the words of eternal life" (John 6:68), and Thomas cries out, "Let us go with him that we may die with him" (John 11:16). They are everywhere we look, it seems, beacon towers swinging their light through the pages of scripture. They are the children at the gate who will not go away and who pray in the only way left to them—with their hearts and their great, spendthrift, loving actions.

It is not remarkable that we find them also in the parables, where they mirror not only the stubborn determination of human beings but the persistent love with which God calls to us. The woman who pesters the judge until she receives justice, the Samaritan who succors his enemy, the shepherd who, against all the logic of the world, leaves his ninety and nine to search out the one stray—all had their real-life counterparts in Jesus' time, even as they do today.

Children at the gate, just as we might expect, also abound among the saints; the refusal to go away is, in fact, almost a definition of sanctity. Saint Therese challenges the Pope, Saint Willibrord's missions fail and he doggedly sets out again, Saint Hugh stands alone against an angry mob—the examples are almost endless. If the kingdom of heaven does indeed suffer violence, it is the children at the gate who take it, not by storm but by passionate besiegement. It is they who know that the world is changed only by great movements of the spirit and that great movements of the spirit begin—as they must always begin—with one dreamer.

We all live, it seems, on the ragged edges of life, but the children at the gate do more. They pitch their fragile tents on bedrock; they do not live in hope but in the determination that God, by some winter alchemy, will forge light from darkness. They have a high success rate because they never give up and never go away. Amid our well-ordered and proper existence, they are the rebels who refuse to move along quietly.

The children at the gate understand Advent, for Advent is, after all, not so much a time of waiting and preparation as it is a time of transfigured patience, a cry into the night that demands an answer. The children at the gate do not always love themselves—they are often too concerned with other loves—but it makes no difference, for God knows them, loves them, and keeps them.

Our God is a God who also never goes away.

DREAMING IN THE SPIRIT

T he scriptures tell us that "without vision the people perish" and, in another place, "your old men shall dream dreams and your young men shall see visions" (Joel 2:28).

When I first saw the latter quotation, I thought it was quite reasonable and correct. Surely, I thought, it is the young who see visions and the old who are lost in dreams. Since then I have come to believe that the prophet may have had it backward.

The dream comes before the vision because the vision is the shaping of the dream into reality. The dream of Advent comes, and must come, before the vision of Christmas. The dream is the product of one mind, one heart, one spirit; only when it is taken forth and shared with others can it become a saving vision. Only when the dream finds its reality in the world can it heal with power.

The artist dreams the image but only when he puts paint to canvas can it become vision. The composer dreams the music but only when she puts notes to paper can the pianist or the orchestra begin to play. The statesman dreams of peace but only when he can draw others into his dream will the treaty be signed.

It has been said, and said truly, that we are the dream of God. If so, then God's dream of humanity must find its reality, must become vision, in human flesh. The dream of peace, justice and love must, for us, come true in human terms or not at all. The vision has been shown to us and we have been drawn into God's dream.

Now when a human dream becomes a visionary reality, a strange thing happens: it begins to change. As the artist paints, the vision grows under his hand; as the composer works, new and more beautiful sound patterns begin to emerge; as the statesman confers with others, his own dream becomes larger.

The ancient Welsh bards called this living movement of creation the *awen* and in pagan times believed it was the direct voice of the gods; after the coming of Christianity the *awen* was said to be the inspiration of the Holy Spirit. Whatever the origin they believed, these early poets attested to one undoubted fact: the movement from dream to vision to reality is not simply a matter of transcribing an idea complete and unchanging into words or paint or musical notes or boundaries on a map; it is an integral and ongoing part of the vision itself. As has been said, life is not in the candle nor yet in the flame, but in the burning.

It is to this white and holy burning that we are called. Our vocation as Christians is to walk away from the weary mummeries of our day and dream large dreams for the times to come. We must go to the place where the vision begins and bring it into being, and we must go there with our eyes open and our hearts ready. And—a warning—we must steel ourselves to put aside all dreams that are not true and pure and holy.

For it is a sad fact that not all dreams are good dreams. Hitler, after all, dreamed of a master race and showed his dream forth to a nation so deep in agony and despair that many accepted it as a saving vision. With that as an object lesson, we must take care to refuse any dream not based on love, any dream that brings harm, any dream that excludes, in the certainty that such dreams are not from God.

When we have done that, we shall be free to go forward wherever the dream and the spirit may lead us, and to turn that dream, whatever it may be, into vision. It does not matter if the dream is large or small. Francis, believing that God had called him to "build my church," set to work with stones and mortar; Mother Teresa began with no goal other than to ease and comfort the dying homeless of the Calcutta streets. Small dreams have a way of becoming large visions, and when they do they carry whatever power and impart whatever courage may be needed. When we loose the arsenals of the heart, there is no doubt nor fear that can stand against them.

And we shall find the joy that sings in the heart of time, waiting for the vision that will set it free.

LIVING THE LONGEST NIGHT

I n Advent we say we are waiting for Christ to come, but this is clearly not so. We all know perfectly well that Christ has already come. The baby was born two thousand years ago. It isn't a secret any more.

Well then, we say, how about the second coming, the one with power and clouds of glory? Perhaps—but for most of us the second coming is a theory, not an expectation. The end time, once thought to be imminent, has stretched itself over twenty centuries now, and we simply expect it will continue to do so.

We are not waiting for Christ; Christ is not away somewhere planning his return. Christ is always coming, always here.

We are the ones who are preparing and it is not an easy task, for in order to let Christ enter our lives, we must open our full humanity to his full humanity. We must welcome the full spectrum of human experience; we must accept passion, joy and terror as he accepted them.

Today on this shortest of all days, this longest of all nights, we need to talk about pain.

Now I am not a person who believes that pain is, of itself, redemptive; it is far more likely to crush the spirit than to exalt it. Yet it is a fact of human life, a part of the common ground on which we stand.

I remember a time not long ago when I was afflicted with the inflammation known as tendonitis which, though blessedly confined to one hand, was painful enough to keep me awake through several of the longest nights I had ever experienced.

I wish I could say my prayers were noble or even articulate, but in fact they were merely variations on the theme of "please . . . make it *go away."* Compounding the pain was my awareness that mine was, in fact, a very small pain indeed. Outside my window, in the unseen world stretched around me, there were abused children huddling in dark corners, beaten and sobbing women, and terrified, neglected old people. There were men and women dying of agonizing diseases and prisoners twisted by torture. There were many suffering not only physical pain but the far more profound pains of loss, despair and betrayal.

I tried to gather them in. I tried to hope that, if there had to be a given amount of pain in the world, mine might ease someone else's. It was a hard hope to hold onto. They were very long nights.

I do not pretend to understand pain, though for me as for everyone, it exists. I have heard that there are persons who, by some flaw in the nervous system, do not feel physical pain. They live in constant danger, for they can cut or burn themselves seriously and never be aware they have done so. And I think the same is true on a spiritual level: if we walk blindly through the pain of the world, refusing to open ourselves to it, then we shall damage ourselves badly.

Certainly Christ never did so; if anything is clear in the Gospels, it is that he felt the pain of every human he met as if it had been his own. And if we are to carry the Christ life within us, we must do the same. This is not an easy thing to do; it will ask much of us.

We must walk out in all our vulnerability into the midst of everything that God has made and everything that humanity has made. We must look on the beauty of creation because that will show us the extravagant love of God and on the beauty of the things humanity has made because that will show us the swiftness and grace of the Spirit. But we must also see evil and the pain that grows from it because—if we give ourselves to God's purposes—that will show us the healing power of God.

We cannot stand aside because Jesus never stood aside. We must let the pain of the world into our lives, always knowing that it will shake our hearts and rack our spirits—and that there, in the midst of it, we will find the Christ at work.

WORKING THE NIGHT SHIFT

I n the long journey of the spiritual life, there is a night shift and, as Evelyn Underhill notes, "sooner or later we are all put on it."

Nothing could be more true. Saint John of the Cross wrote of the "dark night of the soul"—but John was far advanced on the mystic way. What comes to most of us is the Dark Night's lesser cousin, the religious blues. This too is the night shift and we all come to know it.

The spiritual life, once so exciting, becomes flat and stale. God is far away, hidden in darkness somewhere behind the stars, and God no longer answers our call. "Perhaps God never did answer," whispers the small voice in our minds. "Perhaps God is not and never was. The universe fell into being by some cosmic accident; Christ was a foolish prophet and no more." We pray and find only darkness. We meditate and find our minds tracking old tasks and old worries instead. Where God once filled us with happiness, we now feel only a vast emptiness. We wonder what we have done, we ask where we went wrong. There is no answer.

This is the night shift. Sooner or later we are all put on it.

There are a number of theories about the night shift. The first and most commonly held, of course, is the God-is-testing-me theory which, when you think about it, is quite illogical. Why should God, the God who created each of us as a unique human being and knows all there is to know about us, need to test us as if we were a new-model washing machine? God already knows our strengths; God already knows our breaking points.

If there is any testing going on in the night shift, it is not because God needs to know about us but because we need to know about ourselves. We need to know that we are stronger than we think; sometimes we need to know we are weaker than we think. God uses the night shift to demonstrate ourselves to ourselves. This theory may carry a hint of punishment-for-your-own good, but it has the advantage of logic.

The third theory is the psychologist's theory: God is still with us, still hearing and responding to our prayers. It is we who, like over-ambitious athletes, have worked ourselves into a spiritual burnout. When we have rested and recovered ourselves, all will be well.

Certainly these last two theories have a great deal of truth in them. The spiritual life does indeed demand self-knowledge. In one of her essays, Dorothy L. Sayers cites the legendary curate who prayed fervently, "O Lord, teach us to take our hearts and look them in the face." Honesty—ruthless and hard-nosed and passionate—does not come easily to human beings, yet it is essential to our ongoing life with God. Not only that, but maintaining it requires a good deal of mental energy.

In the same way, we give ourselves most fervently to God when all is going well. When we walk in what seems to be endless sunshine, when the loving presence of God walks with us speaking of goodness and mercy and love, then indeed we often overextend ourselves. Prayer is a delight; we forget that it is also a psychic and physical drain. The night shift may well be psychological burnout, but if we are wise we will learn from it that we need not be aware of God's presence; it is with us no matter how much our feelings may waver. Prayer need not be delightful to be effective.

As for me, I have often wondered if the night shift may perhaps be a necessity of our lives with God. We are coming to understand more and more that all creatures on this planet are interwoven in a great and complex web of being; if this is true of our physical lives, then should it not be true of our spiritual lives as well? If we have been taken into the life of Christ, we have, by that very commitment, volunteered to take our turns as guardians of the perimeter. We have been asked to stand steadfast in darkness and hold the line for all those within, and until this particular duty comes to an end, we wait where we are placed, if not with joy then at least with patience and courage.

Unknown and unseen, God stands with us. And I think perhaps, unheard in the dark, God whispers, "Well done."

THE LORE OF LOVE

I n Advent we too are called to incarnation. We bring our humanity to the manger, not to be changed or done away with but to be transfigured. This will require much of us. If we are to live the Christ life to its fullest, we must strip away many things but we must also let in many things. The last and greatest of these things is love.

Perhaps it may seem strange to speak of letting in love as if it were a difficult thing requiring a great effort. After all, love is something we all want; we want to give it and we want to receive it. And we know that love is the one thing God asks of us.

Yet the love of God is a hard, true thing. We are not called to have warm and gentle feelings. We are called to love God "with all our heart and with all our mind and with all our soul" and to love our neighbor as ourselves. This is not a mild suburban demand. This is not a task to be done with ease. True love is the act of a will that is both disciplined and brave.

For the great secret of Christianity is that it is not—and most emphatically is not—a religion of law. There are no rules and regulations. There is only the command to love.

There seems to be a natural desire in human beings to find—or make up—rules and then follow them. The reasons may be many: the need to be at one with our companions and colleagues, the need to be careful in an uncertain world, the need to smooth the workings of the multitudinous institutions and societies and corporations we have made. I also suspect there is a good dollop of human laziness in the mix—if we follow the rules well enough, we may never have to think about what we're doing and why we're doing it at all.

In the spiritual life, following the rules may lead us into a trap we never suspected, the trap of believing that if we live properly and in accordance with all the rules, then God will make everything All Right.

But things are never all right. This is a dangerous and inconstant world and there is no human life that does not have its share of both joy and tragedy. If we think in terms of pleasing God so that God will be good to us, then when the bad times happen, as they will for all of us, we may either think that God has betrayed us or that we ourselves have failed; we were good but, for reasons we don't quite understand, we were somehow not good enough.

And none of this has anything at all to do with love.

We are not asked to be good but to love as God loves—a love bountiful as sunlight, given without reserve and without condition—and such love does not come easily to us. Our hearts are ambivalent and unsure; for us, love is entwined with power and possessiveness, with our need for security or comfort or a dozen other things. Letting love into our lives means putting aside many of our dearest psychological treasures—our anger, our judgmentalism, our jealousies, our pride, and all the other needs that we have convinced ourselves are necessary parts of our identity. Letting in love may also mean putting aside such real and deeply felt essentials as our own hurts and sorrows.

Yet every year we replay the great demonstration of true and unfailing love. The scene at the manger is a scene of spendthrift love, love willing to risk everything, love without measure.

We have Mary, a young woman ready to risk ostracism, or even death by stoning, in order to do God's will. We have Joseph, whose love was stronger than all the feelings of doubt and betrayed pride he must have felt. We have shepherds and wise men—simple folk and sages—watching their lives undone and yet still coming to worship before this gift of innocent light.

And of course we have the baby himself, the baby who will become a man, become a preacher, a teacher, a condemned criminal, and, finally, our model down all the centuries for unconditional love.

We now stand at the day before the night before Christmas. It is time to become one with those shepherds and wise men. In this last gentle time, let us love God and our neighbor, and let us not neglect to love ourselves as well. Let us drop behind us like empty waterskins all that hinders us and all that troubles us, knowing that love will provide a purer water.

In this last day before the coming of the child, let us keep our lamps burning, our lives at peace, and our hearts ready to be filled.

THINE ALMIGHTY
WORD LEAPS DOWN

T here is an old monastic prayer for Christmas Eve: *In the night, when all things lay in quiet silence, thine almighty Word, O God, leapt down from heaven. . . .*

Forget the rather eccentric theology, which would seem to suggest (and may have been intended to suggest) that the eternal Word and the infant Jesus were joined only at the moment of birth. Move past the poetry, that striking image of the cosmic Christ leaping down like a meteor, a dazzle of light destined to burn a short time on the earth. This small song of praise keeps us in mind of a great Christmas truth: the Christ and the child are one.

Tonight we have reached the stable, the place we have been moving toward through all the short days and long nights of Advent. In this season when we let the great mystery of the incarnation enter our lives, we now take the final step. We welcome the Christ child. Not simply the Christ and not simply the child but both, and both together. The Christ and the child must be joined in us as they were joined in Bethlehem.

First, I think, we must speak of the child, for when we open ourselves to the child within us, we open ourselves to hope. No one can hope as fervently or with as much faith as a child. Hope and expectation are the core of childhood. Everything lies head; almost nothing lies behind. Children dare to hope for the impossible, and when the impossible comes true (as now and again it does) they greet it with wonder.

A child is open to the world, a child is curious, a child lives in the world of "what if . . ." A child knows that change and adventure are a part of life and welcomes them. A child believes the best of the world.

A child is filled with trust. No one trusts like a young child, no one has such belief in goodness. The world will teach its lessons soon enough; by the time we are adults—if not sooner—we have learned better. We learn that hope is often disappointed and that many of the things we want most desperately are impossible. We learn to close ourselves away from the world; we learn to protect ourselves. We have learned that trust can be betrayed. And when we learn these things the child in us dies, no matter what age we may be.

We become fearful and distrustful; we lead lives without hope. We accept the world as it is. The child is gone and we cannot find it again.

But when we let in the Christ child, we let all these things back into our lives. We let in the knowledge that God does not accept the world as it is, the knowledge that God has sent us the Christ child so that we may be healed of our fears and our pain. God has restored to us the most extravagant hope of all; God has sent us the Christ child so that we may love in a way we never could love before.

For in the Christ child there is more than hope—there is also strength to grasp that hope. This is the strength of Christ, and in it we lay hold of hope and transform it into dream and then into vision.

In the Christ child there is more than trust. There is also a spiritual power that not only believes in goodness but lays hold of it and shapes it into reality—sometimes in unlikely places and among unlikely people.

In the Christ child there is more than openness and curiosity. There is also courage, the courage that allows us to go forth in love, undaunted and unafraid.

To welcome the Christ child into our hearts is to welcome all our desperate and impossible hopes and to know that they have come true.

It is to welcome hope not as a possibility but a reality. It is to know that we have been given strength, we have been given the power of the Spirit, we have been given the courage of God so that out of that strength and that power and that courage we may be free to love as God created us to love—not in some vague future but now, here, on this holy night and for all eternity.

This is the night of all nights when we celebrate the gift that has been given, the gift that is ours to keep forever.

FIRSTBORN OF ALL CREATION

T his is the day of all days when we see that the God we worship is no narrow God, not the God of this small earth, but the God of the cosmos and that without the divine fiat there "was not anything made that was made" (John 1:3). We are a part of the plan of a God who is the God of all the universe.

The Christian religion is profoundly incarnational. Not only do we believe that the Word was made flesh and dwelt among us—the eternal Logos, the son of God, became human—but we ourselves are spiritual beings and flesh and blood beings, each nourishing and sustaining the other.

Now to live incarnate—in flesh—is to make choices, to walk one road and not another, to accept the consequences—good and bad—of choices that much of the time we make without knowledge or wisdom. It is to know that the past is gone, the future is not yet here, and the present moment is the only moment in which we can truly act.

And yet we are also living in eternity. Paul writes:

For [God] has made known to us . . . the mystery of his will, according to the purpose which he set forth in Christ as a plan for the fulness of time, to unite all things in him, things in heaven and things on earth (Ephesians 1:9–10).

This is the great vision of Paul: the time is coming when all things will be united in Christ, when the joy and splendor of all creation will shine with the glory of union with God. As he walked the hard roads of the first century, Paul knew that moment was coming toward him, that every step he took, every word he spoke, every day he lived brought it nearer.

And we know the same thing. The kingdom is coming. The union of all things in Christ is on its way and every hour, every moment brings it closer. The thing that was begun in Bethlehem is being worked out down the centuries. We do not know how long it will take; we only know what the end will be.

Now Paul, in another context, says that Christ is the firstborn of all creation. And if Christ is the firstborn of creation, then we Christians could well be called the firstborn of this union with Christ, this union of all things in him. Because we are already united with Christ by baptism, we become the forerunners—the shock troops, if you will—in a struggle that will end only when, in the fullness of time, God is all in all.

Our lives are defined by Christ. By being what he is, he makes us what we are. He is the door that opens to us the mystery of what it means to be human. He is the light by which we see ourselves. Because he is the human Christ, he shows us our humanity. Because he is the cosmic and eternal Christ, he shows us what God intends for us and for the universe. Because he is the firstborn of creation, he shows us what creation is meant to be. And he calls us to be united with him in the work of bringing all things to himself.

There is a passage in the writings of Saint Therese of Liseaux in which she meditates on the Old Testament passage, "Draw me and I will run." She writes: "O my God, if you draw me, I will run to you. And all those I love will be drawn with me."

The only thing God wants from us is that we love, because by our love we draw all creation nearer to its divine center.

Do we need any greater evidence of how much God has loved us? After all, Christ could have saved us and left us to go our ways. He could have given us ease and comfort and spared us any kind of suffering. He has not done that. He has made us his body and with our hands he will reach and save, with our eyes he will weep, with our minds he will create justice, and with our tangled and uncertain and loving hearts, he will shape the future of all creation.

THE DAY AFTER THE DAY BEFORE

The mad yearly rush of the holiday season has ended and, quite suddenly, we wake up and find ourselves becalmed in the post-Christmas doldrums. We are, quite simply, tired. The clergy is tired, the choir is tired, the Sunday school teachers are tired. And the average churchgoer is tired too, tired of attending services, tired of holiday get-togethers, tired of crowded schedules and special events.

We are all tired together and amid these many lows, the lowest of all is our energy level. We have simply approached religious burnout, and we need time to sit back and think about it all.

This is, for that very reason, a dangerous time, for at such times we tend to look out on a bleak world and somehow we feel that this infant, whose coming as our savior we have just celebrated, achieved very little. The world seems to be rolling grimly on and evil and despair still rise up to strike at us. The old sorrows and the old griefs track us like relentless hounds. Life is never easy.

And, of course, it might have been. God could have chosen to make a world where nothing could go wrong. A world with no wars, no natural disasters, no injustices, no famines. There would be no earthquakes to topple cities, no bombs to crush the innocent. Perhaps wood might be strong and sturdy when we wanted to build houses and churches and schools and turn soft and useless when we wanted to use it for bad purposes, such as hitting each other on the head with it.

Our very tongues would be affected. We would be able to say kind things but find ourselves speechless when we started to utter angry words and pass along cruel gossip.

Would any of us want to live in a world like that? A world completely without freedom, a world where our every action would be judged before we could perform it? We would be God's toys—we would be dolls in a doll-house world. A world without love, for without free will, love becomes a meaningless enforcement.

God did not make a doll-house world. God made a hard, harsh, beautiful, free world, filled with danger and joy. And God made us to live splendidly in that world—not in the splendor of wealth and power but of generous and noble hearts and free and fearless minds.

God made us to be Christ's companions in glory. God made us to share in Christ's saving, healing, and redeeming work.

And can any of us look at the world around us and not know that savers, healers, and redeemers are needed? God made a world that is free—and therefore contains the possibility of evil. Human beings have all too often taken that possibility and turned it into reality.

Everywhere on God's world we see minds that are slaves to prejudice and anger, hearts that are filled with bitterness and hate, lives that are twisted and broken. And everyone we see—every child growing up in bitterness, every lonely, hungry old person, every broken, hopeless man or woman—is a life Christ came to save.

Paul wrote to the Corinthians: "We have the mind of Christ" (1 Corinthinians 2:16). When we see wrong in the world it is not for us to wring our hands and say how dreadful it is. It is for us to do what Christ would have done: to move outward and set ourselves against whatever evil we may see, to stretch our hands in healing, to redeem hatred with love.

Just as Christ freed the boy possessed by a dumb spirit, it is for us to free the unfree; as Christ healed the lepers, it is for us to heal the broken in body and spirit; as Christ led the disciples up the mountain to see his transfigured glory, it is for us to lead others toward the wholeness and freedom of God.

This may sound like more than ordinary human beings can do—and it is. But we are something more. We are human beings who have the life of Christ living within us. "We have the mind of Christ," and the mind of Christ can not only dream a great dream of human freedom, it can also—over many years and in many thousands of places—begin to make that dream into reality.

Let us never refuse to see the truth, and the truth is that we are faced with great evils, we are faced with terrible needs, we are faced with wastelands where there is no love. And we—we here and now—have been called to go forth under his banner.

We do not go alone. We are gloriously companioned by all who have heard God's word and answered it. They ride with us now. We are the companions of Christ himself.

A HUNDRED CIRCLING CAMPS

I n a passage in the Gospel of John, Jesus speaks to the disciples, say-ing, "The servant does not know what the master is doing; but I have called you friends" (15:15). It is an amazing statement, made more so by the fact that in the ancient world a disciple was indeed expected to function as a servant, searching out food and shelter for his master, carrying his belongings when they moved from place to place and otherwise seeing to all his needs.

Yet Jesus (as usual) fails to follow tradition. Over and over in the Gospels we see that we are never to be servants. We will never simply be told to follow orders; we will never be told not to ask questions. We are friends, with all the joy and tension that relationship carries within it. We are beside God; we have seen the battle plan taking shape; we are told what we are doing and we are told why.

Paul writes: "For [God] has made known to us the mystery of his will . . . to unite all things in him, things in heaven and things on earth" (Ephesians 1:9–10).

This is the Christian vocation: to unite all things in God, to heal all things in God, to redeem all things in God. We are all part of the living body of Christ and therefore we are part of God's plan for uniting all things.

I remember the day this first became real to me. A friend and I had attended a Commission on Ministry conference, and for both of us it was a powerful experience; we came away knowing we had begun the journey. We went to church knowing we had given ourselves to God and that God would take us and use us forever.

That was the week the Anglican bishop was murdered in Uganda. I didn't know then that a few years later I would meet one of the priests who had been with him, a priest he had ordered—on obedience—to go away while he himself stayed to face death.

And then, at the same service, we baptized a baby and there, quite suddenly, was the church, spread out through time and space and eternity, praising God for the faith of one who had come to the end and—almost in the same breath—consecrating a new life to Christ. And I stood in glory and awe and wonder at our blessed company of all faithful people, doing simply and matter-of-factly what it has done for twenty centuries and will do as long as God wills it so.

The early church believed quite literally that we are all one in Christ and that it is Christ who lives in us. We have read his righteous sentence and we have builded him an altar, and if we are a bit bewildered at having been drawn into the redeeming mystery of the incarnation, then so be it. Our God is the God of the unexpected, the Lord of wonder and vast surprises.

We have been called to the great work of redemption and this means that the one thing we cannot be concerned with is our own piety, our own righteousness, or even our own salvation. We are called to the healing of a world that is badly in need of it. We pray and every prayer we utter is a prayer from within the body of Christ; every prayer draws on the riches of every other. And this is so not because of our abilities but because the grace of God has willed it.

We are called to be holy, not for our own sakes but for the sake of the world. The theologian Jorg Splett recently wrote that we are living in "a time of sanctity without glamour." When we look around our world, we can see that it is so. The Christians who are struggling in Africa, in the eastern nations, in our own inner cities, are not concerned with glamour but with hard realities. They deal with sweat and ignorance and human pain and sometimes with violence and death. Sanctity is not glamourous except from the outside.

And yet sanctity is our calling—sanctity and all the courage that is a part of it. We are called to love, sometimes when love seems impossible. And God takes whatever we can give and uses it for the healing of the world. We are a part of the continuing incarnation of Christ, irrevocably intertwined with all the others, past, present and, in the light of eternity, those still to come. We are joined in the life of Christ, and God gathers all we are and all we do into one great mystery of love, healing, and redemption.

SLEEP IN HEAVENLY PEACE

S urely "Silent Night" is the most beloved of all the Christmas carols. It is one of the first we learn as children, a simple song charged with nostalgia and illusion. I have heard it sung by a famous contralto in a packed cathedral, in Spanish by an Hispanic teenager in a small darkened church, by a homeless woman with no accompaniment at all, only her pure, sweet voice rising in the cool air.

It haunts us, this song that is fixed so deep in us it seems to murmur in our blood, this music that is also the memory of a dozen childhood Christmases, this dream of an impossible peace that, for the moment while we sing, lies over us like a great, warm garment. The greatest of all possible gifts has been given and we have laid claim to it. There is nothing more that we can ask.

For this one moment we can forget that tomorrow we can and will ask for a great deal more; tomorrow we will also remember that the child whose birth we celebrate knew little peace, lived in violent times, died by torture. Tomorrow we will be back in the world as it is, the world of Stephen and John and slaughtered children. We have been promised the peace of God, the peace that passes all understanding. Where did it go? And where shall we find it again?

The answer, of course, is that it has not gone anywhere; it surrounds us, waiting for us with the vast patience of God. It is we who have looked for it in all the wrong places.

For the peace of God is not contentment nor warm physical well-being, nor even the absence of strife. This peace is not as the world gives; this peace lies on the other side of struggle; this peace lies beyond the hard winter journey and the cold stable, beyond Gethsemane and beyond the cross. This is not an easy peace. It is found in wounds and despair and defeat; it is a costly peace. It is also a peace with power in it.

This power is the power of God. Jesus says, "As the Father has sent me, even so I send you" (John 21:21). Evidently we are to lay hold of this peace that is so unlike what we have imagined, and we are to carry it out into a world that exploits and kills its children, a world that knows nothing of peace at all. And we come to understand that this peace of God is neither rest nor ease nor comfort. It is the helmet on our brow and the banner in our hand.

"If you want peace, work for justice," says a recent poster. How can there be peace in a world where human beings are treated only as markers in a war game, where many are exploited so a few may be rich, where children are denied the simple birthright of food and shelter and love, where the beauty and dignity of men and women goes unseen behind ethnic and color barriers?

This is the world to which we are commanded to bring God's peace, the peace we have been promised. "If you are to give it away," says a character in Charles Williams' novel *Descent into Hell*, "then you had better have it first." This is a truism when spoken but an enormous difficulty in practice. How shall we find this peace of God, this peace that comes in power so that it may be our flag, our armor, and our gift?

I think perhaps we may begin by singing our dream of heavenly peace not only for the baby in the manger but for all the children of earth, dark and light, Christian and non-Christian. By singing the vision especially for the hurt, the broken, and the slain. By carrying the song out of the church, knowing that it calls us not to personal comfort but to struggle, and that only within that struggle will we find the true peace promised by God.

The peace that the world gives is a sheltered, sweet peace, and what the world gives the world may take away. The peace of God is a battle harness, and it is not given but won at a price. We are called to know God's purpose, to see God's vision, and, having seen, to bring it to all creatures. The harness is justice and the banner is courage.

In the end, we will see that they were only the other names of love.

GREAT CLOUD OF WITNESSES

The world seldom knows its saints. A few are recognized during their lifetimes and liturgically commemorated afterward, but they are the exceptions and not the rule. It doesn't matter: God knows them all.

One day we will know them too, and we will find with joy that they walked among us, that they were our friends and neighbors, our fellow churchgoers and our colleagues at work. In a glory of recognition, we will cry out, "It was you! You who once helped me and never told me. You whose prayer gave me strength when I most needed it. You who eased my grief . . ." Then we will know one another, not as the ordinary people we meet and talk with and work with every day but as shining and noble spirits fit to consort with angels.

Not only will we recognize others—we will also recognize ourselves. One of the hard truths of the spiritual life is that we rarely see any result. We give our work and our prayers and our lives to God, and God uses them in ways we seldom see. There is no greater act of faith than to go on working and praying, in darkness and sometimes in pain, when God seems not to hear us, and yet that is what we must do. The work God does in our lives and through our lives is almost always unseen and unknown.

All we can know is that we are not alone. We are companioned by all Christian souls, those living now and those who have gone before; perhaps, in the mystery of God's will, those yet to come walk with us as well. We are surrounded by what the Letter to the Hebrews calls "a great cloud of witnesses," and what we all witness to is the action of the incarnate Christ among us. The life of the eternal Christ incarnate in time continues in us and defines our lives. We live in its light and by so doing we share in the saving and redeeming purposes of God.

We have been gathered into God's act of healing, an act that embraces all the world. We are not merely recipients—we are active participants. I always feel a little sad to hear someone talk about "being saved" as if there were no more to be concerned about. Christians are not charged with oversight of their own salvation but with the salvation of all the world; as we heal and care for one another, so in the all-embracing reaches of the divine economy shall others heal and care for us. However small our contribution may seem, redemption is our vocation.

Once we have accepted our place in the body of Christ, we will never again be alone in the great work in which each one is held and supported by all the others. We may feel like lonely sentries holding a barren outpost all by ourselves, but even in our deepest darkness we are held and sustained by the great multitude of souls in which Christ lives.

Never again can we say that what we do doesn't matter. Our part may seem to us to be very small, but that is not for us to judge. "Pick up a pin for the love of God," says Saint Therese of Liseaux, "and you may draw a soul into the light." Our workaday steadfastness may make the difference between an outpost held and an outpost abandoned. What we do *does* matter, and for all we know it may matter infinitely.

We cannot understand this great community of Christ unless we understand that Christ did not do his work and leave the world behind. Christ is living and working now; his work continues to find its human shape in us. The transfiguration of the human soul has a far larger meaning than our own personal salvation; it is a part of the movement of the entire universe in its return to the Creator who set it into being and who with tireless love calls it home.

THE LAUGHTER OF GOD

H appy families are all happy in much the same way," Tolstoy writes in the opening of *Anna Karenina*. "Each unhappy family is unhappy in its own way." With due respect to a great writer, I think Tolstoy has it backward. God laughs in the happy family and therefore love and laughter take a million different forms. Unhappiness is always and everywhere drearily the same.

Recently a friend and I sat over coffee and congratulated ourselves at our singular good fortune in having been born into happy families. Our two professions, different as they are, have shown us both dysfunction and its aftermath. We had long ago realized that the warmth and caring we never questioned is, in truth, beyond the hopes and even the imaginings of some children.

"Of course," said my friend thoughtfully, "my family was a little bit nutty."

"Mine too," I said and we both laughed and lost ourselves in stories of the aforesaid nuttiness, remembering things we hadn't thought about for years, things neither earth-shattering nor life-changing except for the warm balm they spread across our memories.

It is a very good thing to be born into a nutty family.

My particular memory was of the late winter when my father and his younger brother decided to make root beer. Why they decided to do this remains a mystery, for no one in the family was overly fond of this old-time beverage. Still, it was a Project, thought up in a dreary and boring time of the year, and it was valued as such.

The Project (as Projects often do) turned out to be much more complex than had been thought, entailing the purchase of an enormous pottery crock, a number of glass bottles, and an equal number of metal disks, as well as the rental of a complicated gadget for pleating these disks onto the tops of the bottles.

When the great day came, the crock was hoisted onto the kitchen table and the ingredients measured and stirred, an operation that required the stirrer to stand on a stepstool and lean down like an angel across the bar of heaven to confer with the groundlings. There was the realization that no one had remembered to get a funnel and the dispatch of my uncle to fetch one. There was a certain amount of argument and mild cussing before the cap-pleating device could be made to work.

At last, however, the Project was accomplished and, rank on rank and file on file, a small army of bottles stood at attention along the kitchen counter, each wearing a small golden cap and looking quite promising.

At the time, no one suspected that we had produced a regiment of artillery.

I remember that I was quite disappointed that we could not drink the root beer at once. It was necessary, it seemed, for it to lie for six weeks in a cool, dark place while the yeast—an important ingredient that had been much fussed and argued over—did what yeast does and produced a froth of bubbles. The little army was banished to the basement and the family admonished to go there seldom and turn on as few lights as possible, lest the slumbering root beer be disturbed.

Four weeks passed, and then almost five, until the night when, as we sat at dinner, we heard beneath our feet a small but definite explosion and the tinkle of broken glass.

"Something fell over," said my mother hopefully. "It might be a burglar," said my grandmother. "I think," said my father glumly, "that a bottle blew up."

And so it had. In the week that followed we lived above an intermittent bombardment of exploding root beer. When the time was up, my father daringly rescued the few surviving bottles and we opened them and drank them up before they too could go the way of all glass. The root beer itself was something of an anticlimax.

We never discovered what made our root beer so volatile, though it was much discussed. At any rate, the Project became a family legend but never a family tradition: once was enough.

So I think maybe Tolstoy was right after all; happy families are alike in their nuttiness.

Perhaps this is what makes them happy families—their tolerance of benign impulses, their good-humored acceptance of one another's foibles, their willingness to laugh rather than blame. There may be argument and anger from time to time, but there will never be rejection.

In the rigid and controlled family, we learn a love that is contingent on proper behavior; in the happy family (the nutty family, if you will) we learn a love that is broad as the sky and unconditional as sunlight.

And of course the place where we learn about love is also the place where we learn about God.

MILLENNIUM THREE

How long have we been in the third millennium? The fact is that we don't know; there is simply too much variance in dating systems, too much argument among scholars as to the exact year of Jesus' birth for us to claim that any given year marks a millennium.

Even so, a new year marks a milestone where we may pause a minute, wipe our brows and perhaps sit for a time looking back along the road we have traveled and making such plans as we may for the journey yet to come.

It has been a long and rocky journey so far, filled not only with great branchings of the road but also with false trails, dead ends, and a number of quirky little bypasses. It is hard to see all of the road—there are too many obscure turnings and hidden curves—but one thing is certain: we have come a great deal further than we often realize.

Some years ago I ran across a story in the writings of an early Greek author—Plutarch, I think—telling of a rich man who found one of his most valued possessions missing.

He immediately accused his slave of the theft and—apparently being a man of high temper and little sense—had him beaten, bound hand and foot, and thrown into a ditch. "But wait," said a friend on learning of this, "perhaps the slave is not guilty," and eventually the slave's owner agreed to investigate further.

He accordingly did what nearly every Greek of his time would have done: he journeyed to the shrine of Apollo at Delphi and proceeded to ask the oracle if the slave was indeed guilty. No, he was not, the priestess replied; the slave was entirely innocent. The man hurried home and rushed to the ditch to free the slave but, alas, travel was slow in those days of mules and ox carts; too much time had gone by and the slave was dead.

The Greek author presents this cautionary tale complete with moral: if the man had not been so hot-tempered and hasty, he would not have lost his valuable slave and had to buy another. The story gives us not one word about justice, not one word about the value of a human life.

This is the sort of world into which Christianity came and in which it existed during its formative first years, though it is undoubtedly no accident that it had its genesis in Judaism, a religion unique in that day for its insistence on just treatment of slaves and charity for the poor.

So we have made progress, slow though it may be. Justice is still seldom served, but we have come to believe that it ought to be. Human lives are still wasted wholesale, but we have come to believe that they shouldn't be. We live in a world that, until comparatively recently, accepted wars as inevitable; today we still have wars but we have begun to ask why.

We have lived through what I believe will be called the Century of Liberation, and if there are still flaws and inequities to be sorted out, we have at least begun to assume that we must do so. As we begin to deal with Millennium Three, we find ourselves, rather startled at the newness of it all, in a time and place where no one will ever again hold power by keeping the people in ignorance, and if www.com seems to be a modern version of the tower of Babel, we have confidence that we will tame it.

There may be arrogance in this and there is certainly danger, but there is also upward movement. If ever there was a time when we needed to keep our moral values focused on unconditional love and our strength and courage ready to hand, it is now. If ever we needed to moved swiftly and surely from dream to vision to reality, it is now.

For Millennium Three will test us as we have not been tested before. It will require us to look at our worldwide society with a cold, clear eye for both the ills we see and those we do not yet see. And it is not going to allow us the years—even centuries—to deal with them that we had in the past.

We have made mistakes and will make more; we have lost God's dream and found it again many times. There is no failure except giving up the struggle.

God has shown us the vision and given us the free will to follow it. And God walks with us into the future.

NOCTURNAL FOR THE NEW YEAR

T he new year has come. We have celebrated in whatever way seemed good to us, observed, or failed to observe, whatever family traditions we may have inherited, wished each other a happy new year. Now the parades and the games are over. We sit amid the dregs of the holiday season. Within a few days we will again be immersed in our work, our families, our hobbies, our favorite TV programs.

It's over. Why does it seem so ordinary? Is the future after all going to be much the same as the past?

Whatever the future holds, we know this about it: it will come to us one second, one minute, one hour at a time. This moment, like every other moment, is the point-instant where the future begins. The future, whatever it may be, will be shaped by acts of God, by other human beings, and—not least—by ourselves. The God who created each one of us a unique individual has also gifted us with inviolable free will, and by this gift made us partners in the creation of ourselves.

God creates us with potentials, but it is we who make the free choices that bring those potentials into being. God created us to love, but it is we who allow that pure and holy fire to burn within us and, if we refuse, God will not force it upon us. We were made in the image of God the creator, but if we choose to destroy, God will not prevent us.

God has given us an enormous gift, the gift of being co-creators, and what we create is the one person each of us was meant to be. That is the work that we take up on this night of new beginnings, as we take it up on every other day of our lives.

And make no mistake—the job of creating ourselves as true and complete human beings is indeed *work*. It is not something that will happen by itself. It is not something we can leave to God, for God will never override or take away our moral choices.

Is it any wonder that we sometimes become discouraged and sometimes even believe we have failed?

But in the largest sense we do not and cannot fail; we can only give up the struggle. Because this is true, I'd like to give us all, on this first night of a new year, not resolutions but wishes. And, as is the age-old tradition, there will be three of them.

First, I wish us all to be a little unsatisfied. The world is very old and very strong and when we look around it, we know that we are very small. It's easy to say, "This is the way things are. There is nothing I can do." I do not wish any of us that kind of peace. I wish that we may always see the flaws in ourselves and in our communities, not so we may criticize but so we may heal. I wish for all of us not only the ability to dream, but to dream greatly.

The second wish is that we may all be a little bit stubborn. I know that there are nicer words—words like "persistent" and "determined"— and if anyone prefers a gentler synonym, then by all means use it. Whatever we call it, we are going to need it. There are times in every life when we need to go on, no more than that and no less. Go On. And there are also times when we need to resist. There is evil abroad in our beautiful world and for the true man and the true woman there cannot be any compromise with it. We will need all our stubbornness when we come to stand wherever God may place us.

The third wish, of course, is essential: I wish us all strength and the courage that goes with it. If we are to dream greatly and make the dream come true, if we are to see evil and stand against it, then we will need all the strength we can find. And I wish us more than courage—I wish us the high gallantry that is the birthright of all who go forth under Christ's banner. I wish us the gallantry of those who know the world has no defense against a love that does not surrender and no defeat for those who stand firm in faith.

May God go with us all.

GRAVEYARDS

In a western state there is a graveyard where someone dear to me is buried. It is a small graveyard atop a rise of rolling land that might, by some stretch of the imagination, be called a hill. Long prairie grasses blow around the gravestones. A dirt road borders one side and a row of pines, bent nearly to right angles by the prevailing winds, lines the other.

Beyond the pines stands a small, abandoned church of indeterminate denomination, as was common in frontier towns. You can still unlatch the door, go inside, view the rough-hewn benches where the worshippers once sat and the black, big-bellied stove that warmed them. The occasional meeting of one community group or another is still held here, for old times' sake, but there are fewer of them each year. Many other warm, well-lighted places—with softer chairs—are available.

The graveyard itself remains stark and unkept. Few burials take place there now, though the rare sentimentalist—like my dear almost-aunt—still opts to lie with his or her forebears. Most of the graveyard was filled before the frontier ended, before the cities came.

The gravestones have felt the effects of time, the hard wind, the blinding winters, and have begun to lean at strange and eccentric angles. All are made of the same tough grey granite, the sort that is not so much hewn or carved as simply battered into shape by brute force, and almost all were clearly carved by the same person, some local stonecarver who made up for ineptitude and poor tools with a certain breezy nonchalance.

It was a time and a community that favored long biblical quotations over short and pithy epitaphs. I imagine that town stonecarver crouched in his shed by night, lantern carefully placed, beating letter after letter into the unforgiving stone.

He probably had few tools beyond a hammer and chisel; certainly he had none of the power-driven equipment wherewith a modern carver might tame this stone. These old letters waver and cant from side to side like the land itself. When the quotation was too long for the space allowed, our stonecarver was not bothered at all. He calmly continued the line around the side and onto the back, or made a sharp right-angle turn down the margin. To read these stones you must twist your neck to the side, or walk around them while the relentless wind blows and the long, hard grasses slap and clutch at your ankles.

This is a good place. The last time I saw it (a long time ago, it seems) I sat in the shade of a stand of glassberry bushes. Summer wildflowers bloomed in the ditch beside the road, with a few diligent bees trundling back and forth among them; none had any inclination to brave the noonday breeze to investigate my hilltop and I was grateful. I sat and let the warm wind and the deep prairie peace wash over me.

A boy came down the road leading a calf, walking without hurry through the sweet, dry sunlight, taking advantage of a bit of broken fence to shortcut across the little graveyard. The calf, young and barely broken to lead, balked and the boy slapped its rump, raising a small, golden cloud of dust. They departed through a gap near the pines and went their way, leaving me as enchanted as if I had seen an angel or a saint.

How fitting, I thought, how fitting that they should appropriate this place, should make it their own, even for a shortcut. The dead will not mind. Life goes on and those who lie here once knew it.

There are moments that come rarely and unasked, that cannot be made or bought or bargained for, when we understand that nothing lives alone or to itself. Bee and boy, calf and woman, glassberry bush and summer flower, wind and grass and living earth, all sing together, caught and made free in the matrix of life where time slides away and where past and present dwell in the eternal love that, as Dante well knew (having also traveled this road), "moves the sun and other stars."

WALKING THE WALK, PRAYING THE PRAYER

S ooner or later we all ask one another, "How do we pray?" How do we go about this thing that is, after all, the center of our life with God? Prayer is the channel of our communication with the divine, and yet we all seem to feel uncertain before it.

Well, the temptation, of course, is to reply, "Any which way you can." As long as we come into the presence of God sincerely and with open hearts, there is no wrong way to pray. Prayer is a dialogue of love and trust and as long as we have those three things—dialogue, love, and trust—we have prayer.

Perhaps the hardest of these is trust. We understand love and we also understand that prayer is not simply a recitation of our needs and desires but a process of communication. But trust is more difficult for us.

This is where the Hebrews in the desert went wrong. God had brought them through the Red Sea; God had heard their cries in the agony of slavery; God had brought them out of Egypt; God had led them to freedom. Within days, faced with thirst and no water to slake it, they are murmuring, they are doubtful, they are rebelling.

God provides water.

Now the food runs out, and the murmuring begins again. Now the people are angry and even begin to wish they were back in slavery. Slavery is safe. Slaves must be fed in order to work and every slave-holder knows it.

God provides manna and quails.

But the same thing happens again. I've always felt very sorry for Moses. The poor man is only trying to do what God has called him to do, and everyone is shouting against him. And the reason for it all—as we and he can easily see—is that they have lost their trust in God.

This, I think, is the main point of the story. God can be trusted. God will hear us. God will part the Red Sea. God will make the waters pure; God will provide whatever we may need. And we who come later, we who have been called the Easter people, we who are gathered into the life of Christ, often have the same problem.

We don't really trust God. We have a lifetime of learning that we can't always count on human beings and we transfer that distrust over to God. The Blessed Julian once wrote that we accept that "God is all-knowing and may do all, and God is all-powerful and can do all, but that God is all-loving and will do all—there we fall short."

So when we pray, we begin with trust that God will hear us and God will answer us. God may not answer in the way we want—true—but God will always answer in the way that is best for us.

Such trust isn't easy. We live in a secular society and a consumer society. We believe, because we have been told from birth, that we should have anything we want. It's not easy against that background to get down on your knees and put your total trust in a supernatural being you can't even see.

But no one ever said it was going to be easy. Remember the Samaritan woman at the well? Life wasn't easy for her either, but when Jesus tells her about the living water that quenches thirst forever, she has only one reply: "Sir, give me this water."

And for us, too, this is the first step: to come to God in love and trust that the living water is there for us as it was for her, as it was for the Hebrews in the desert, as it is there for everyone simply for the asking. It's as simple—and as hard—as that.

When we trust in God's unfailing love, when we ask not for this or that but only that God will come to us, then God has demonstrated again and again in scripture, in the lives of Christians past and present, in our own lives, that God will come to us with a speed that leaves us staggered.

In truth, however, it is wrong to speak of God coming to us, for God has never left us. It is our own willingness to trust and to open our hearts that makes us aware that God's love surrounds us, as universal as sunshine, as close as the air we breath.

All we have to do is accept it, take it into ourselves, and give ourselves to the fullness and mercy of that love.

THE PRINCE, THE GARBAGEMAN, AND THE DOG

An ancient story, so old the only copy is written on papyrus rather than parchment, tells of a prince born to the throne of some distant desert land. In good folklore form, his birth is attended by a prophecy: he will be slain by a dog.

The queen and king, of course, are horrified, and all dogs are immediately banned from the kingdom. The prince grows to manhood without ever seeing a dog or even being told that such a creature exists. The time comes, however, when—again in good folklore form—the prince must set out on his hero's journey, the quest that will save his land and people. Of course he meets a strange creature and the courtiers who have come to see him off cringe in fear: "A dog!" they cry. "A dog!"

Despite their warnings and their hand wringing, the prince remains firm; he and the dog have bonded as only true friends can bond, and he insists that this new companion will make the journey with him. The two set off alone, into the desert.

And there the papyrus breaks off. The rest of the story is lost.

I, too, when I was rather younger, set off on a hero's journey of sorts. My quest was for fame and fortune and my goal was to conquer New York City which, in the event, declined to be conquered. I ended with the sort of grim job that pays the rent (barely) and keeps you fed (not too well). A broken shoe heel was an emergency of epic proportions.

Each morning I boarded a bus crammed with people whom I suspected of being no happier than I. Jammed together and all swaying as one, we lurched *en masse* up Lexington Avenue and, such was the excellent timing of this bus, at the same place each day we passed a garbage truck.

Now New York garbage is massive and varied and much of it is noisome. As I watched the unfortunate minions of the City of New York slinging this fetid stuff into their truck, my first thought was that here were people doing a job (impossible thought) worse than mine.

My second thought was the depressing reflection that, however perfect and utopian our society might one day become, it would doubtless always need garbage collectors.

My third thought was the realization that one of these workers was quite remarkable. He was a very large black man with a smile like sunshine; he laughed, he joked, he tossed canfuls of garbage into the compactor with the aplomb of a master athlete. Simply to look at him brightened New York's sunless canyons.

It goes without saying, I suppose, that he made other people happy, but that is not the point here. The point is, rather, that this man had discovered an enormous secret, a secret he shared with the prince in that antique folk tale: Life Is. All we can do is live it with real tears and real laughter and as much grace as possible.

Life is simple, so simple it often gets away from us, slipping its leash and bounding off like a large, joyous dog while we remain shouting and fuming and chasing after, determined to make it settle down and *behave.*

The dog cares not at all for what could be or what should be and certainly not for what might have been.

So, to turn our folk tale into an allegory, the dog is life and the prince is all of us and we write our own endings to the old tale. In one version the prince heeds his advisors and shuts himself away in a palace tower, where he lives a long and quite meaningless life.

In another version, he goes forth, running in dread from every dog he sees and living in fear that one day the fated dog will catch and eat him, as of course—in good allegorical fashion—it one day does.

In the last version, he goes forth with the dog; he makes a friend and companion of life and death and chance and destiny. Let us assume that the dog guides him well, so that he achieves his quest and returns home with the magic sword or the flower of eternal life or the Holy Grail. It does not matter, for he and the dog have seen wonders and enchantments, seen beyond the sky and into the deeps, followed the hidden trail into the mountains of the spirit. And when at last the dog kills the prince, as in the end it must, it is not the end of the story.

It is the beginning.

ON EARTH AS IT IS IN HEAVEN

I f you were to gather every Christian from every denomination in the world, how could you get them all to pray together? Quite easily—you would say the Lord's Prayer. The languages would be different, of course, and even among the English speakers there would be a small cacophony on "trespasses . . . debts . . . sins" and the Roman Catholics would drop out on "For thine is the kingdom . . . ," but these are small matters. This is the prayer everyone knows, the first grownup prayer we learn, the prayer we say every time we attend a church service.

When I was in seminary, one of my fellow students did hospital visiting for a local parish. One day as she reported the comatose condition of a terminally ill woman, the rector asked if she prayed for her during the visit. "Of course," replied my friend. "I say a silent prayer before I leave her room."

"Next time," said her rector, "pray out loud."

Feeling rather foolish, she did so, reciting the Lord's Prayer at the bedside of a patient who had shown no sign of consciousness for several days. To her utter amazement, she looked down and saw that the woman was silently forming the words with her.

Such is the power and universality of this prayer, and yet its very familiarity is a danger. How often do we gabble our way through the words with little thought to their content? What do we mean when we speak of "Our Father who art in heaven"?

Well, if we had been born in the Middle Ages, that question would have been a good deal easier to answer. Everyone knew where heaven was. Somewhere above the clouds, God was sitting on a golden throne. God was wearing a crown and royal robes; just as any human king was accompanied by a crowd of fawning courtiers, God was surrounded by a retinue of angels and saints.

Today we have become more sophisticated. We have journeyed to the topside of the clouds and beyond, and not one scepter or golden throne have we seen or expected to see. British theologian Charles Williams suggests that we may enrich our prayer if now and again we pray, "Our Father in whom is heaven," simply to remind ourselves that heaven is not a place where God dwells but, rather, wherever God is, there is heaven.

And God is everywhere. No corner of this seemingly endless universe is so distant or so small or so obscure that God does not enter it, love it, hold it in being, and fill it to overflowing.

Heaven is not far off, heaven is not above the clouds, heaven is not a place where we go when we die. Heaven is here and now because God is here and now. We walk through heaven every day of our lives, though all too often we don't see it. Heaven is where God is, and when we pray that God's will may be done "on earth as it is in heaven," we are praying an extremely complex prayer.

God, we believe, is pure holiness, pure goodness, and pure love. We further believe that it is God's will that we share in that holiness, goodness, and love. But we also look around us, as intelligent and spiritual beings should, and we see that something seems to have gone disastrously amiss with this idea. God's will is clearly not being done in the realities of this world.

We look for a reason—and a reason is not hard to find. Perhaps the Blessed Julian of Norwich said it best when she wrote: "For all our travail and all our woe is naught but the failing of love on our part." Whenever the holy seems far away, whenever the kingdom seems not to come, whenever we're sure God's will is not being done, this is the first question we must ask: "Where is the failing of love on my part?"

We cannot single-handedly cure all the profound evils of this beleaguered planet, but where is the failing of love that keeps us from doing what we can? For when we pray this passage from the Lord's Prayer we are not praying simply that we may know God's will, but that God's will should be brought into being in this world. And we pray that, as we seek out the failings of our love, we may more perfectly become the agents of God's love to all around us.

We are God's children, clothed in God's light. We are God's dream, we are God's plan, and the task love sets before us is to know that God's kingdom is here and God's kingdom is now and that we—by our love and forgiveness and healing—will do our share in making it visible on earth as indeed it is in heaven.

THE THIRTEENTH DAY
OF CHRISTMAS

The twelve days of Christmas are over. Our revels now are ended. For most of us, they ended some days ago and we are deep in the workaday world again. We probably began packing away the decorations a week ago. For those who insist on a real tree, that tree is already a memory; in these commodity-driven times, most trees are cut too early to last beyond the new year. The cookies and candies have all been eaten and we are planning our spring diets.

As in poet W. H. Auden's phrase, "we have tried unsuccessfully to love all our relatives." We are ready and more than ready for a taste of the humdrum. We have two more months of winter to deal with and we need to get on with it.

Today the wise men have arrived. Good for you, guys. Glad you could make it. Better late than never.

Meanwhile we have an odd little season that can't make up its mind whether it's white or green and has little other than kindly old bishop Valentine to enliven it. It once had some wonderfully quirky names for its Sundays (remember Septuagesima and Quinquagesima?), but those have somehow been lost under the feet of a pragmatic and hurried world.

Yet this strange little catch-all season is one of the most important in the church year and deserves much more attention than is usually given to it. It is the last Christmas present, saved until now, and today—the Feast of the Epiphany—is the day we unwrap it.

The Epiphany is the "showing forth." It is the time when, having been given the gift of the incarnation, we are invited to fold back layer after layer and examine with care exactly what we have been given.

This gift of incarnation is no simple gift to be placed on a shelf and admired. It is complex, intricate, and mysterious. Like a turning prism, it blasts pure light into as many colors as the eye can see and undoubtedly some that it cannot. Like a finely tooled machine, it demands not only our examination but our participation in its purpose. And, in the final analysis, we discover that it has not been given to us to keep but to give away in great prodigal handfuls.

The wise men brought gold and frankincense and myrrh, the traditional and symbolic gifts of kingship, godhood, and death. None of them, of course, was of any use or interest to a child, but humans, like God, can only give what they have and, ultimately, all any of us have is ourselves. The wise men brought the gifts that were themselves and received the gift that was God's self, which is the same gift, rushing forth in endless abundance, that we all receive.

Were they, too, surprised by this gift of infinite complexity? Did they turn it and touch it and wonder at its meaning? Were they, like us, astounded to discover that by these gifts—given and received—they had been drawn into nothing less than the showing forth of the Christ? Did they protest that they had been caught unguarded and unready, or that this gift in the shape of a child was too great for them? Did they, protesting their unworthiness, try to give it back?

But God does not take back a gift once given. We can refuse it, perhaps we can even smash it to bits, but we cannot return it. Nor are we ever worthy or, for that matter, ready. The gifts of God come gently in the night or blazing like Moses' bush at high noon, but they are never given as rewards or bestowed as prizes; they are as unconditional as the Godhead itself.

That is why this peculiar little season is so important. In this season we examine the gift—not simply the gentle image of the baby in the manger, the kindly animals, the kneeling shepherds and at last, today, the wise men with their swaying, bad-tempered camels and their swift little desert horses—but the gift in its entire meaning, shown forth to the world.

In this season, we explore the meaning of incarnation in our own lives, we study this thing that has happened, this physical joining of God with the created universe, this "taking of the manhood into God" and if

Christ's manhood then all of humankind, drawn into God and linked to the Godhead forever. This thing willed in eternity is now shown forth in the only way we can comprehend it—in flesh and in time.

This is the thirteenth day of Christmas, the long day that we will live for the rest of our lives, the day in which we, who are the body of Christ, show forth the Christ who now dwells in us.

We are the epiphany.